AF552459

MODERN TEACHING OF HOME SCIENCE

MODERN TEACHING OF HOME SCIENCE

[Strictly According to the UGC Syllabus for B.Ed. Course]

By
Fahmeeda Begum

ANMOL PUBLICATIONS PVT. LTD.
NEW DELHI - 110 002 (INDIA)

ANMOL PUBLICATIONS PVT. LTD.
4374/4B, Ansari Road, Daryaganj
New Delhi - 110 002
Ph.: 23261597, 23278000
Visit us at: www.anmolpublications.com

Modern Teaching of Home Science

First Published, 2004

ISBN 81-261-2106-8

PRINTED IN INDIA

Published by J.L. Kumar for Anmol Publications Pvt. Ltd., New Delhi - 110 002 and Printed at Mehra Offset Press, Delhi.

Contents

Preface

Education is a vast discipline and Teachers' Training is a vital part of it. The responsibilities of the educationists and educators are focused on the task of providing better training to the future teachers for their better learning and proper development. Needless to say that this responsibility can only be exercised, if the trainers are equipped with the required knowledge of the subject concerned. That's why it becomes essential for making adequate provisions for each course to the student-teachers or teacher trainees. The present series is designed for providing a solid workable base for all course-papers. It has been prepared strictly according to the syllabus of the B.Ed class, prescribed by the UGC for different universities.

No doubt, there are so many other books on the subject, available in the market, written by worthy authors. However, every writer has his or her own style and way of presentation. The present work also has its own features and characteristics.

In preparation of this series of texts, the editor had to refer to the works of other authors and information sources. The editor feels a deep sense of gratitude for incorporating their ideas in the text. Hopefully, this series would serve as a 'ready to refer' tool for all teachers, teacher-students and others.

—Editor

Preface

Education is a vast discipline and teachers' training is a vital part of it. The responsibilities of the educationists and educators are to work on the basis of providing better training to the future [illegible]. Better training and proper development [illegible] [illegible] that this responsibility can only be exercised if the trainers are equipped with the proper knowledge of the subject concerned. That is why it becomes essential for making adequate provisions of each course for the training of teachers or teacher trainees. The present book is designed for providing a solid and useful base for all courses. It has been prepared strictly according to the syllabus of the B.Ed. class prescribed by the UGC for different universities.

No doubt, there are so many other books on the subject available in the market written by worthy authors. However, every writer has his or her own style and way of presentation. The present work also has its own features and characteristics.

[illegible] of this [illegible] the editor [illegible] grateful to the [illegible] and other authors and information sources. The editor feels [illegible] [illegible] suggestions in the [illegible]. [illegible] are [illegible] readily to offer [illegible] for all [illegible] teachers, students and others.

Editor

1

Introduction

Home Science education covers a broad spectrum of science and technology, human development, child care, health, nutrition, housing, clothing, conservation of energy, post-harvest technology, waste disposal, protection of environment, handicrafts, dyeing, printing, weaving etc. The specific goals of Home Science Education are to improve the:

Conditions contributing to spiritual, psychological and social development.

Conditions contributing to health and nutrition development.

Physical components of existence and quality and an availability of services which enrich family life.

Home Science education integrates modern scientific knowledge with the cultural and spiritual traditions of the past, thus making home life a source of happiness and strength for the family. Research in this field needs to be oriented towards awakening the community, safeguarding the interests of the people and helping them to improve their ways of life.

The effects of a rapidly changing society on the family and the effect of home and family life on the quality of working life are deep rooted. At this stage, the role of Home Science becomes very crucial.

The need for an education that addresses the perennial concerns of families-food, clothing, shelter and human development is ever present. Home Science is an ideal discipline for helping families manage human and material resources.

Home science can prepare individuals and families for long, full and effective participation in the community, taking note of the social and technological changes taking place. Career planning, life planning and consumerism can be considered integral part of the mission. The components, then, must be personal development, personal and family resource management and career planning. The process can be introduced to help students in decision making and problem solving.

A major issue that assumes global importance is pollution, a byproduct of development. Man's continued actions towards progress and his constant interaction with nature have not only disrupted the intricate balance among ecological constituents but also polluted the essential resources for sustenance of life on this planet. Significant progress in this direction can be achieved by incorporating environmental ethics as a component in the Home Science curriculum.

Women's role in economic process is an important feature of national and international forums. Women at present are employed in the labour force of textiles, electronics, agribusiness and in other spheres. In order to sustain the pace of development, efforts should be oriented towards expanding women's opportunities that result in enhanced productivity and earning potential. This will improve their living standards and contribute to economic progress, reduction of poverty and increase of family welfare.

Presence of computers and other electrical appliances in the home have immense implications for the family in new appliances, in concern about energy consumption and management, in housing availability, in new food products and processes, in new fibres and fabrics for clothing and for interiors, in skills needed by the young in order to cope with daily tasks.

Much of the labour force works in the creation, processing and distribution of information which influences a major section of the activities.

The production and marketing of information, products and services all qualify for the entrepreneurship concept. Home Science expertise in child care, care of the elderly, developmental programmes for the handicapped, marketing of food and textile products have potential for economic benefits.

About 70 percent of the people in India are engaged in agriculture. On the production of land depends the success of the national development plans, growth of industries, enhancement of the family standard and education and health of the people.

Agriculture forms the backbone of the Indian economy and occupies a place of pride. There is a heavy responsibility on the agricultural sector to produce food to meet the needs of the population both in terms of quality and quantity and also provide employment to a large section of the population.

Women, particularly studying Home Science, can play a very important role in improving the agricultural production and conserving the produce for national security. Some thoughts on the agricultural aspects for the Home Science curriculum can be like this.

There is need to have a glimpse of the growth and development of the nation through Home Science programmes operating in the field of health, agriculture, education and technology. Foundation courses in Home Science can be supplemented with interdisciplinary subjects, to equip the present generation to meet the future challenges. Realising the importance of youth in nation building, Home Science can contribute to building up a strong youth forum. They can be trained to develop a favourable attitude towards service to the society and nation.

The uniqueness of Home Science lies in the fact that it is the field of study with the nucleus of the family as a social and economic institution and the individuals who function in that direction.

The welfare, health and full development of every citizen is the moral responsibility of the modern state. It will not be possible without population control. Thus, the specific problems and examples dealing with population dynamics can be introduced at various levels of the Home Science curriculum.

It has been estimated that oil resources will exhaust in 50 years, the coal resources in 100 years. From the middle of 21st century man cannot depend on oil and coal. Thus, there is an urgent need to find viable solution to the growing need to find energy. Home Science can teach the women about the application of non-conventional and renewable energy. For this, various energy management and conservation strategies need to the studied and educated.

Home Science has its priority goal centered on the concentrate personnel and financial resources on education related to the survival needs of the nation, the alleviation of starvation and malnutrition, prevention of family disharmony and violence, procurement and maintenance of shelter for protection, support for caregivers of dependents, reduction of financial risks and effective consumer decisions regarding management of resources.

2

The Significance

The study of Home Science is the study of "home and family". An ideal home can be considered as a heaven on earth. The holiest temple is not the building used for the worship of a God but the home, the first school for the child. Right education begins emotionally and not intellectually. The emotional education of the child begins at home. The early education of the child is in the hands of his parents and his family. Because of this, Home-Science has been introduced as a separate subject of study in all the centers of learning. With the study of Home Science man learns the truth about how to live and how to treat our fellow-men and how best to utilise the different resources of our country. The origin of home is as old as our country. The origin of home is as old as our civilisation and so is Home Science.

Home and House

Historically, civilisation began with the origin and development of the home. Home thus made start in the history of mankind. In the beginning he started staying in cave and afterwards he learnt the art of home-making and since then home became an integral part of human life.

The concept of home differs from person to person, country to country and age to age. There is a difference between the primitive home and the modern home. The Indian home is not the same as an American or an English home.

Ordinarily 'Home' and 'House' denote the same thing but truly speaking there may be a 'House' which is not a 'Home'.

'Home' is the place where a social unit called family comes into existence. A family comes into existence when a man and a woman decide to marry to satisfy their basic wants, they achieve this fulfilment and the children grow up to adulthood in continuance of the life cycle.

A 'House' is a mere structure which provides shelter and protection from the elements of nature.

Indian Home

Indian home was dominated by and is still dominated by philosophical pursuit. The philosophy that originated in vedic ashrams has been preached and practiced in the Indian homes. In accordance with this, an Indian is expected to pass through four stages i.e.

Brahmacharya: At this stage he gets education and prepares himself for his future life.

Grahyastha: During this stage a person leads the life of a householder.

Vanaprastha: During this stage he is expected to lead a life of retirement and meditation.

Sanyas: It is the stage when man is required to lead a life of renunciation.

It is hoped that while passing through these four stages, attains the four-fold aims of life i.e., (i) *Dharma*: or the attainment of moral values. (ii) *Artha*: or wealth, (iii) *Kama*: or enjoyment of desires, and (iv) *Mosksha*: or liberation for attachment of sufferings.

The home, according to the Indians, is another name for woman, the mother and the wife. In vedic society perfect equality with man was granted to woman. They enjoyed such rights and many a woman studied the vedas and some of them even became vedic 'Rishis' and teachers of vedas. Some such names to mention are those of Lopamudra, Ghosha and Yajenvalki. Actually speaking in ancient India, woman were deified. They were considered as 'Shakti' the energy behind Lord 'Shiva'. Women gives up her life so as to bring a new life.

In Indian scriptures, home has been defined as "arihini griham uchyate". This means, "the mistress of home is the home". To further emphasise it the Indian husband is asked to utter the following `Mantra' at the time of marriage, "come and become the queen of my house-hold". Women pay various roles in home as a wife, as a mother and as a sister.

Importance and Value

With the introduction of a course in Home science it has become the programme of the people and by the people. It has helped in the planned, conscious development of home and family.

Its aim is to provide the intellectual, cultural, moral, aesthetic, vocational, utilitarian, economic and social values not only to the individuals but to the society as a whole. The study of Home Science has also initiated and directed a burning desire to achieve higher standards of living and the will to live better. Some of the important values of Home Science are as follows:

Vocational Value : The knowledge of Home-Science provides an opening to many a professions. It also forms the basis of many a courses of study which is purely vocational in nature, such as dietetics, nursing, teachership etc.

It has helped to solve the problem of leisure as the study of Home Science forms the basis of many useful hobbies and other productive activities in the later life of the students.

Foundation of Good Citizenship : Some of the requisites for a person to be a good citizen are as under:

Pre-planning, adjusting to the environment, proper use of available materials and resources, importance of realising human relationship, sensitive to cleanliness and learning by doing etc.

The study of Home Science helps to inculcate these values to the pupils. The curriculum in the framework of instructions. The Home Science syllabus provides various opportunities to the students for completing the work, allotted to them in time and thus prepares them to be good planners, efficient executives and responsible leaders. They are expected to come forward and accept various responsibilities in the school.

Home Science is based on arts and sciences. Purity in personal life, devotion to the family and simplicity which are considered to be the glorious attributes of Indian womanhood are the basic foundations on which the art of Home Science rests.

Universality : Home is the basic social institution that has existed since times immemorial. It is a primary social group that is charactrised by a common residence, cooperation and reproduction. In spite of great scientific and technological advancement, the most modern and civilised society of the day has not been able to give a complete and fully satisfying substitute for home. So we can say that the origin and development of home is of universal nature. It can, therefore, be concluded that the teaching of Home Science is universal.

Self-reliance : While going through the course of Home Science a student has to rely on himself/herself. Her own judgment, reasoning and initiative alone is of use to her at every step. It thus develops self-reliance in her.

Solution of Household Problems : We know that the two basic factors that have an influence on personality development of a child are heredity and environment. By environment we mean home, parent, family, friends, surroundings, food, clothing, education, relation etc. Though the effect and interplay of various environmental factors are a complex process and so we can not easily say which one of the various factors of environment plays a more decisive role in shaping the character of an individual. With the study of Home Science we acquire the ability to give each of environmental factors its right place and proper emphasis. Thus, the study of Home Science helps in solving many a domestic problems.

Preparation for the Change to Come : In the olden days, girls learnt house-hold work by example and practice and there were no special arrangements in the form of formal courses in home-making.

In the present times, though the home-making has been modified yet it basically remains unchanged. These days Home

Science occupied an important place in the educational curricula of all grades from nursery school to the university level.

As General Education : Home Science education is quite helpful in preparation of homemaking, in the development of right values. It also makes a contribution towards increasing health and happiness and enable to pupils to understand the functions of parenthood, responsibilities of family membership and management of one's resources. Thus if the aim of education is the preparation of life then Home Science has a tremendous scope for general education. It is considered as one of the important subject for girls in high school stage. In its report the Secondary Education Commission points out that the present day education does not confirm to the objectives of general education, especially, in case of girls, and that education should be more closely connected with the home and community. Therefore, they have urged that the teaching of Home Science in girl's schools is essential and home making should become an integral part of educational background to girls.

Preservation and Transmission of Culture : Good homes and good communities are basic to democracy. Homes also determine the production, distribution and consumption of wealth in a society. Homes help to preserve and transmit our cultural heritage from one generation to another. It is Home Science which enables the students to know the importance of home in providing emotional education to the child right from the day of its birth. This education humanizes the family and the society.

Economic Importance : In the modern times, a large number of women seek careers outside the home. This may be due to economic necessity or may be due to the availability of ample leisure time. A knowledge of Home Science provides many an opportunity to such women in various fields. In this way, they can combine home-making with wage earning.

Ability to Live a Richer and Purposeful Life : One of the aims of teaching of Home Science is to create an environment and outlook that enables people to live richer and a purposeful life. Happiness of family is the desired goal of all the activities undertaken in teaching of Home Science. The teaching of various topics such as family health, nutrition, home-improvement, child care, textiles and clothing etc. all are directed towards the goal of happiness of family.

Contribution of Home Science to School Organisation : By 'organization' we mean 'to arrange things in an orderly manner'. Teacher of Home Science helps us in enrichment of various activities in the school and in this way contributes towards the efficient organisation of school. Some such activities are given below :

Area of Home science	*Contribution to School Activities*
Nutrition	(i) Maintaining a record of heights and weights of students,
	(ii) Arrangement of kitchen,
	(iii) Arrangement of store-room,
	(iv) Cleaning and storing food,
	(v) Planning menus,
	(vi) School garden activities,
	(vii) Storage of drinking water.
Household management	(i) Cleanliness and orderliness of class-rooms,
	(ii) Cleanliness and maintenance of library,
	(iii) Planning and maintenance of accounts,

Contd.

Area of Home science	*Contribution to School Activities*
	(iv) Planning of exhibitions and leisure time activities.
Textiles and clothing	(i) Selection, purchase and storage of textiles,
	(ii) Construction of clothing, school uniform,
	(iii) Laundry work,
	(iv) Dying and printing,
	(v) Stain removing.
Child development and mother craft	(i) Preparation of dolls and toys,
	(ii) Games and sports,
	(iii) Stories for the young.
First Aid	(i) Sound health habits,
	(ii) Cleanliness,
	(iii) Knowledge of first aid.
Human relationship	(i) Good citizenship,
	(ii) Cooperation and friendliness,
	(iii) Organisation and celebration of festivals.

Thus, we conclude that in addition to its educative and economic roles, the teaching of Home Science inculcates the following qualities in the pupil.

(i) It provides an emotional basis for home.

(ii) It attempts to meet the demands of modern times.

(iii) It helps in the scientific study of home management.

(iv) It prepares women to adjust themselves to social change.

(v) It helps for appreciation of values.

(vi) It creates proper attitudes.

(vii) It develops ability to solve household problems.

(viii) It provides the knowledge of proper habits and skills.

(ix) It helps in the preservation, promotion and transmission of culture.

(xi) It contributes towards school organisation.

Philosophy of Education

Ours is a vast country having a rich cultural heritage and to preserve this heritage, she must keep herself in tune with the changing times. She has to look to the development of science and technology in such a way as to bring within her reach much material wealth and the pleasures and leisures. We have seen that the development of agriculture and industry leads to an increase in physical standards. However, it is the life in the home that provides lasting peace and happiness.

Aldous Huxley says, " Men live in accordance with their philosophy of life, their conception of world". Thus, philosophy is valued the individuals to live the best kind of life.

The philosophy of Home Science is the philosophy of 'home and family'. The home is identified with the woman of the house.

Women in Indian homes play a dynamic role as mothers responsible for upbringing of children, as wives looking after the comforts of husband and relatives, as home makers inculcating the faith and strength in the minds of all family members and above all looking to all round development in family life. Manu says, "that country in which women are respected and educated will indeed prosper."

Education is necessary for both men and women because "wife is the half of man". A question that comes to mind is what should be the content and pattern of education of woman? What knowledge is essential to them? Should they receive education for home management?

As an answer to the above questions, it can be said that the basic purpose of women's education should be : (i) to meet the demand of modern times, (ii) to prepare them to face the impact of science and technology on society, and (iii) to promote and transmit the culture and values of the past. To achieve these ends Home Science education is the ideal pattern.

In this regard, one of the main recommendations of the Secondary Education Commission appointed by Government of India was that proper facilities for teaching Home Science be provided in girl's school.

Spafford and Amidon list the following as the broad purpose of Home Science education:

(i) To establish such values which make personal, family and community life meaningful.

(ii) To create a home and community environment that is conducive to the healthy growth and development of all.

(iii) To achieve wholesome inter-personal relationship.

(iv) To use resources so as to satisfy needs.

(v) To developmental understanding and appreciation of cultures and ways of life.

Writing about philosophy of Home Science education, Hall and Paolucci state

" The study of home economics helps the person to develop as an individual: it promotes good mental and physical health and also an appreciation of art and beauty through its concern for guidance and direction of life."

QUESTIONS

1. How can you define Home Science? What is its importance in our life?

2. Can the knowledge of Home Science reduce the drudgries of a housewife? Explain it.

3. Elaborate the concept of Home and how it has changed in Modern times than in the primitive age.

4. What is the importance of teaching Home Science in Today's context? .

3

Aims and Objectives

For the proper teaching of subject it is essential to have a knowledge of aims and objectives of the subject. This is also true for the teaching of Home Science. Various methods of teaching are then evolved according to these aims and objectives. For determining the aims of teaching any subject we have to take into consideration the utility and usefulness of that subject. We have material as well as spiritual aspects in our life. For a successful spiritual life, it is essential that we have a well-founded material life.

The aims and objectives of teaching various subjects are normally very similar and they are generally guided by economic and social considerations. The aims and objectives of teaching Home Science include all the aims and the objects of education. Different writers have listed these aims and objectives in different ways.

In this chapter, an attempt will be made to discuss these opinions.

Aims of Teaching Home Science

Aim refers to the conscious purpose that is kept by us before our eyes while performing any act. It helps us to take stock of the results of our activities. It acts as a yardstick to measure our success or failure in life. The important aims of teaching Home Science are as follows:

Utilitarian Aim : Home Science is a practical subject and it prepares us for a better self of confidence in the young girls so that they can independently prepare their meals.

A course in Home Science also prepares the pupil for different types of employments. It also enables them to choose and construct home furnishings and to recognise the importance of their care and use. They also learn to apply various scientific principles to the selection and use of fabrics. It also helps the students in improving the qualities of leadership.

Intellectual Aim : The main emphasis in teaching of Home Science is one's intellectual development. Home Science emphasises upon originality. Home Science provides a good training in various fields and offers ample scope to exercise intellect which breeds confidence, responsible personality and vigorous energy. It provides the opportunities for taking decision which are based on clean thinking and judgment. Students also state testing their own thinking and that of others they acquire the ability to apply scientific principles for the solution of their household problems. It makes the student self-reliant. They also learn to work independently by applying their intellect.

The Social Aim : Society refers to a compact human organisation. Knowledge of Home Science socializes the girls. They learn to identify themselves with all the members of the family.

They develop sympathetic understanding of human life, mutual faith, mutual adjustment, responsible attitude and a clear understanding of various human problems.

Probably Home Science is the only subject of study which seeks to develop all these qualities required for the efficient functioning of an organised society. By its study, girls become well informed. Of the various new ideas that have been added to the study of Home Science is the conviction that human population must be controlled. It is expected and believed that it is only through the study of Home Science that we will be able to solve this problem of population explosion. It is with this aim in mind that the home scientists have included population education programme in the syllabus of Home Science. Such an educational programme is aimed at developing an awareness and understanding of the relationship between the population growth and national development.

In Home Science, students are expected to learn how the family, school and communication are interdependent and this helps to develop a healthy relationship between the members of the family, school and society. It also helps to broaden the outlook of girls so as to relate the family to the national economy, the national education system and even the national political system.

National Aim : Today's children are tomorrow's citizens. Home is the first school of citizenship. In the present day society, the responsibility of good citizenship has grown enormously and so is the task of schools. The teaching of Home Science aims at developing a feeling for nation. Instead of teaching a child in a different way, Home Science advances vast scope to train the young mind at home. Home does not mean the four walls of the house, it extends into the community of people and nations, the most important contribution of Home Science is to inspire in home makers a desire to serve the nation and to promote international understanding and good will.

Practical Aim : Home Science is a practical subject and is closely related to different aspects of life. It is related to food; nutrition and cookery; housing and home-management; textiles, clothing and laundry; first aid and home nursing; child development and mother craft; Human relationship etc.

In Home Science classes, students are provided opportunities for practicals in almost all the above stated fields of life. These practicals provide them the opportunities to express creatively their talents. They also get opportunities for appreciating the aesthetic and psychological factors in food.

Development of Right Attitudes : Attitudes of an individual depend upon intellectual and emotional factors. Desirable attitudes are based on an appreciation of things which are worthwhile in life. It is the responsibility of Home Science teacher to develop such right attitudes amongst her pupils and for this it is essential that teacher herself show such traits as self-control, sympathy and patience. Scientific attitude refers to an attitude that is not effected by personal feelings and is based on facts only.

To Develop a Sense of Belongingness : To develop a sense of belongingness of the pupil to home, to community, to nation and to the world is one of the important aims of teaching of Home Science, such a sense can be developed in the pupils if they are provided with detailed information about the multifarious relationships that exist. In addition to giving various facts teacher should make it a point to give their correct interpretation and to explain the principles involved. If taught in a proper way the learner feels that she belongs to the family, to the society, to the nation and to the world.

Competence in Solving Problems : At present, we observe a tendency in the students of expecting that for each problem there is some ready made solution available in the book. Such an attitude is playing havoc with the life of the students. However, a student of Home Science always tries to find a solution to any problem by herself. This gives the students self-confidence and they can find solutions to various problems in life.'

Development of Specialisations : Presently a number of job oriented courses in Home Science have been developed. Such courses are referred to as "Vocational Home Science", e.g., dietaritics, institutional management, nursery school teachers etc. The ample job opportunities after such courses will place women in various positions and they will be able to actively participate in various spheres of life. This will lead to the development of an individual in a family as also in a profession.

Development of Research : An important aim of teaching Home Science is the development of research and application, e.g. Teaching of Home Science should help a nutritionist for undertaking research for the improvement in meal planning and management of cooking and food catering agencies such as canteens, messes etc. Research in home management should help to widen its horizon in various ways. To develop improved evaluation methods in Home Science a research is desirable.

Various aims of teaching of Home Science are to be attained during the different stages of education. Some of these may be emphasised more at a particular stage depending upon the physical and mental development of the child.

Aims at the Primary Stage

At this stage of education, a teaching of Home Science should help the pupil to systematise the knowledge received by her from impression at the pre-school stage. She should be familiarised with basic notions and concepts of running a home. This can be done through perception and purposeful action by the teacher.

Stories can also play an important role in this connection. At primary stage more emphasis be laid on systematising the study in nursery and pre-primary stage.

Aims at the Secondary and Higher Secondary Stage

The major aims of teaching of Home Science at this stage of education can be summarised as follows:

(i) To develop a sense of awareness for the art of daily living.

(ii) To provide opportunities for creative expression.

(iii) To develop good work habits.

(iv) To develop individual initiative and self-confidence.

(v) To provide practical experiences in various fields of life.

(vi) To develop a feeling of belongingness to community and to nation.

(vii) To develop international understanding.

(viii) To prepare the girls for their future life.

(ix) To develop in the pupil the proper scientific attitude.

(x) To enable pupil to create an environment and outlook to live richer and purposeful lives.

Enumerating the goals of secondary education the Mudaliar Commission suggests as follows:

1. Developing democratic citizenship.

2. Increasing the productive or technical and vocational efficiency.

3. Developing the personality.

4. Developing the leadership.

The Kothatri Commission said, "Education should be developed so as to increase productivity achieve social and national integration, accelerate the process of modernisation and cultivate social, moral and spiritual values."

The goal of Home Science is the same as that of general education:

(i) Individual security,

(ii) Health and well being, and

(iii) Social and emotional integration.

The knowledge of Home Science can be effectively employed by the pupils

(i) to solve various problems in his daily life,

(ii) to build happy homes of future, and

(iii) to prepare careers outside the home.

The Objectives

The objectives are the specific and precise behavioural outcome of teaching a particular topic in Home Science. Any topic in geography helps in realising some general aim of teaching Home Science. The characteristics of a good objective are as under:

(i) It should be specific and precise.

(ii) It should be attainable.

Bloom's Taxonomy of Objectives : Bloom's taxonomy of objectives is a classification of instructional objectives in a hierarchy. According to it, the specific objectives have been classified into the following three categories:

(i) Cognitive domain objectives,

(ii) Affective domain objectives, and

(iii) Psychomotor domain objectives

The cognitive domain objectives include knowledge, understanding, applications, analysis, synthesis and evaluation

The affective domain objectives include the appreciations, values, attitudes, interests and feelings.

The psychomotor domain objectives include skills.

These have been discussed in brief in the following pages.

Knowledge Objective : To impart knowledge is the basic aim of education and so it naturally is the basic aim of teaching of any subject including Home Science. By imparting knowledge of Home Science to the students it is expected that she acquires a knowledge of terms, concepts, techniques, and principles relating to the subject of Home Science.

Knowledge objective is considered to have been achieved if the student is able to recall and recognise various terms, concepts, facts, principles and processes etc.

Skill or Ability Objectives : These objectives aim at development of certain skills and abilities in the student. The following skills and abilities are intended to be developed:

(i) Experiment skill,

(ii) Drawing and decoration skill.

This objective is considered to have been achieved if the student

(a) fits the apparatus for various purposes,

(b) cleans apparatus,

(c) arranges articles in proper order,

(d) measures volume, weight etc. correctly,

(e) follows the correct order in performing an experiment,

(f) observes precaution while doing cooking, sewing, needle work etc.,

(g) decorates school and home,

(h) observes and records data accurately and systematically,

(i) makes graph, charts etc. from the data available, and

(j) develops ability in cooking, child care, laundry work, treatment of sick etc.

Appreciation Objective : In regard to the objective of development of appreciation of the subject, the following things are kept in mind:

To develop a power of appreciation of achievements in household management and its role in human life and society.

This objective is considered to have been achieved if the pupil:

(i) Shows thrill and excitement at the new innovations in household management, tailoring, laundry, cooking etc;

(ii) Enjoys collecting and exhibiting pictures of household activities;

(iii) Enjoys to look after home management, cooking, laundry etc;

(iv) Shows enthusiasm and excitement in declaring her own experimental achievements in cooking, tailoring etc;

(v) Enjoys to read about achievements and sacrifices of great home-makers or housewives.

Attitude Objective : Attitude objectives consist in the formation of certain attitudes and habits. In this regard, the following are aimed at:

(i) To develop the habit of completing a task systematically and logically,

(ii) To develop the power of concentration and self study,

(iii) To develop clear expression,

(iv) To develop initiative and confidence,

(v) To develop rational outlook i.e. to express opinion precisely systematically and logically without any bias or prejudices,

(vi) To develop the capacity to utilise the subject in day-to-day life,

(vii) To develop the capacity of analysing a problem,

(viii) Formation of behaviour pattern,

(ix) Application of knowledge, and

(x) Generalisations.

This objective is considered as achieved if the pupil

(a) does not accept or reject any thing without valid reasons,

(b) has a keen desire to know how and why of any thing,

(c) is prepared to face hazards in his investigations,

(d) has no hesitation in admitting his mistakes,

(e) suspends a judgement till it is repeatedly confirmed,

(f) remains unbiased while approaching a problem,

(g) considers all the details, and

(h) observes principles of health and hygiene.

Understanding Objective : Understanding objective aims of developing an understanding various terms, concepts, facts, processes, techniques and principles of Home Science.

This objective is considered as being achieved if the pupil:

(i) can illustrate term, principles etc. by giving suitable examples;

(ii) can express the same fact in various ways;

(iii) can locate and correct an error;

(iv) can compare and contrast between related terms and concepts;

(v) is able to classify substances and facts;

(vi) is able to discriminate between allied substances, concepts etc.; and

(vii) is able to identify relationships.

Application Objective : The pupil is expected to apply his knowledge of concepts and principles to new and unfamiliar situations.

This objective is considered to have been achieved if the student

(i) anlyses situations;

(ii) formulates hypotheses;

(iii) tests hypotheses;

(iv) draw inferences;

(v) verify inferences;

(vi) establishes relationships;

(vii) predicts results and

(viii) finds new uses for substances.

Positive Attitude : This attitude is considered as achieved if the pupil:

(i) likes the teacher;

(ii) gets interests in the subject; and

(iii) likes the company of other students of Home Science.

Interest : Development of interest in household pursuits is one of the major objectives of teaching Home Science. This objective is considered as being achieved if the pupil:

(i) engages herself in household activities;

(ii) visits places of household interest;

(iii) reads allied literature from various sources such as books and journals;

(iv) performs extra experiments;

(v) takes an active part in debates etc., involving topics of household management and

(vi) improvises apparatus for various experiments.

Dr. Ellen H. Richards gives the objectives of Home Science as under:

(a) The freedom of home from the dominance of things and their due subordination to ideals.

(b) The use of various resources, made available by modern science, for improvement of home-life.

(c) The simplicity in material surroundings which will free the spirit for the more important and permanent interests of the home and the society.

(d) The ideal home life of today not hampered in any way by the traditions of the past.

Conclusion

The teacher is required to choose some of these objectives according to his topics or students. He has to try suitable methods of teaching as well. These objectives are also to be kept in mind while framing the curriculum.

However, neither the curriculum framers nor the teachers keep in mind these objectives. The curriculum is framed in accordance with the changing needs of the society and developments in the subjects and the child's level is seldom kept in mind. On the other hand teachers try to concentrate on the subject-matter on the one hand and pupils on the other. They want to rush through the course and ask the students to cram up certain facts formula etc. Thus we find that subjects of teaching Home Science are generally neglected, however, certain knowledge objectives are unintentionally followed by the teachers.

QUESTIONS

1. Discuss the aims of teaching Home Science and its current place in the school curriculum.

2. Discuss the different objectives of studying Home Science. Explain the views of different associations.

4

Area and Scope

Home Science is concerned with almost all the field of education that are essential for running a home. Home represents a miniature community in broader sense. In Home Science we learn many things in many ways. The study of Home Science helps the pupils to become effective individuals and members of the family and community. They develop skills of various types and get a clear understanding and appreciation of cultural and spiritual values, which will help them to live more joyfully and efficiently in their own families and in their future homes after marriage.

Traditional and Modern Concept

Home Science is concerned with the primary and indispensable training of running a home. This traditional concept of Home Science made Home Science very narrow in its scope.

In the modern times, the importance of Home Science has been given recognition and Home Science has become an important and prominent subject of study. Now we consider Home Science as a systematic arrangement, both mental and physical, for running individual homes that is likely to result in the place, prosperity and progress of human society. This definition has made the scope of Home Science very wide and has enormously widened the scope of Home Science.

Basic Nature

In a democratic country, education aims at preparing youth for happy and efficient home and family living. A knowledge of Home Science is quite helpful to the students as it enables them to apply their ability and intelligence for solving various problems of their own lives as also the lives of other family members, community, nation and the world. They become ideal citizens. They learn art of home management. They understand the functions of parenthood, responsibilities of family membership and proper management of their resources. In this way they develop a sound philosophy of home living.

Home is the basic unit of life in a community and is a source of spiritual energy. It acquaints the members of a family to know about individual and group morality. It also helps in the preservation, promotion and transmission of culture from one generation to the next. As an economic unit it determines the productions, distribution and consumptions of wealth in society. In this way, children can learn various patterns of living.

One of the important functions of mother is home-making and motherhood. As a mother, she is expected to look after various aspects of family life such as economic, social, spiritual, technical, physical and psychological. She makes a planning for the use of available resources in order to achieve family welfare. She can receive proper training for homemaking and motherhood only from the study of Home Science. Home Science education has been accepted as an important part of education. A study of Home Science prepares youth for home-making.

The Scope

Scope means 'range, limit or extent' so when we talk of scope of Home Science we mean that topics be included for being taught in a Home Science class. An ideal Home Science programme should contain following major phases:

1. Food, Nutrition, and Cookery,
2. Household management,
3. Textiles, clothing and laundry,
4. Child development and mother-craft,
5. Human relationship, and
6. Health, first aid and Home nursing.

Food, Nutrition and Cookery

Food : It refers to anything solid or liquid which on being swallowed is digested and assimilated in the body and keeps it well.

Nutrition : It is the science of foods. It can be defined as 'food at work in the body'. In it, we study various processes whereby the organism ingests, digests, absorbs, transports and utilizes nutrients and disposes off their end products.

Cookery : It is some thing more than a science. It is an art. It deals with the preparation of various types of foods. It requires a good deal of practice so as to achieve a high quality of product with proper use of time, money and material.

All these, i.e., food, nutrition and cookery which come within the scope of Home Science enable the pupil to recognise their importance for healthy living. It is essential, for maintenance of good health, for students to know how to select, prepare and combine foods in nourishing meals.

In this section of the syllabus the pupil learns about:

(i) Personal, family and community food needs,

(ii) Planning, preparing and service of nutritious food,

(iii) Food habits and practices,

(iv) Table manners and services,

(v) Food production, conservation and preservation,

(vi) Food for special occasions and food for special categories of individual, e.g., the infant, the sick, the old, pregnant woman etc.

(vii) Different types of cooking,

(viii) Handling various types of kitchen equipment.

By the study of Home Science one understands the relationship that exists between food, health and personal appearance. To enable the students to live a more useful and satisfying life, knowledge of food, nutrition and cookery should be given to the students.

Household Management

In it we deal with the administrative aspect of family living. By its study, the pupil develops an appreciation of management in the economical use of money, time and energy. In its simplest term we can define household management as "using what you have to get what you want". Household management deals with all the aspects of human life i.e., time, energy, skills, money, equipment, car, jewellery etc. It is expected that a student of Home Science acquires a basic knowledge of the following:

(i) The process of management,

(ii) Household arithmetic,

(iii) Family resources, budget and financial management,

(iv) Work simplification techniques,

(v) Family consumption and marketing, and

(vi) Safety and sanitation hygiene including ventilation and lighting.

By the study of Home Science, the girls get some practical experience in the above fields which later on helps them to save their energy: (i) by distribution work among members of the family, and (ii) by using labour saving devices and modern equipment such as electricity tap work etc.

Textile, Clothing and Laundry

Clothes not only protect us from the vagaries of nature but they are also an asset to our personality. A proper knowledge of textiles, clothing and laundry develops aesthetic hygenic and economic values. Such knowledge is quite useful for house-wives as it will give the pupils a knowledge of:

(i) Appropriate clothing for different individuals on the basis of individual taste and on the basis of seasons,

(ii) Laundering and storage of clothing,

(iii) Preparing the cloths,

(iv) Operation of serving machine, tailoring, needle-work, embroidery etc.,

(v) Washing and cleaning of clothes,

(vi) Use and care of fabrics, and

(vii) Designing of garments appropriate for different occasions.

Child Development and Mother Craft

The knowledge of child development and mother craft is quite useful to would-be mothers. This knowledge comes in handy to them, when they become mothers, and they plan activities and experience for themselves. This knowledge helps the lady teacher working in nursery schools in selection of good storing for teaching. By the study of this particular branch of Home Science the pupil learns about:

(i) physiological functions of human body,

(ii) family relationship,

(iii) care of the child including pre-natal care,

(iv) hygenic principles for the control of diseases and for a healthy life,

(v) growth and development through the life cycle,

(vi) psychological and educational nature of the child, and

(vii) welfare of children in home, school, community and nation.

Human Relationships

It has already been emphasised that family is the basic social unit. In a family the human relationship begins by the process of interaction between its members and house wife is the chief architect in the foundation of this social relationship. To perform this role, it is essential for the housewife to be social. It is also essential for her to know how to adjust to the family and to the community to which her family belongs? If she is trained in this art she can act as a link between the family and the community. It is with these aims in view that the pupils are taught in Home Science classes about individual and group relations, leisure time activities, civic and social responsibilities, spiritual and moral values etc.

Health, First Aid and Home Nursing

There is a saying "Healthy mind in a healthy body". It emphasises the importance of good health and good health is the key to happiness. In Home Science, the pupils are taught the principles and practices of mental health and physical health and to improve their health habits. This knowledge helps them in maintenance of good health for happiness, control of diseases, care of sick, personal grooming, first aid measures etc. It is also desirable for a successful happy family life to teach young girls topics like sportmanship, tolerance, honesty, integrity, loyalties, ethical standards etc.

Conclusion

Home Science enables the students to properly use their ability and intelligence to solve the problems of their own lives and the lives of the members of family, community, nation and the world. They become responsible citizens in a democratic country. They learn the art of home management. They understand the function of parenthood, responsibilities of family membership and management of their resources. Thus, they develop a sound philosophy of home-living. This knowledge gained in Home Science helps to attain the following goals in secondary school:

(i) To help each individual student to lead a more satisfying personal family and community life.

(ii) To learn the proper use of their intelligence and ability to enrich their own lives and the lives of others in the family, community, nation and world.

(iii) To develop the qualities of ideal citizenship.

(iv) To help them in finding solution to various home and family problems.

(v) To provide the students with guidance and the opportunities to grow up in the social graces, managerial ability and competence in house making skills.

(vi) To become earning members of family.

(vii) To educate them about how to nurture and take care of the young to foster their health, growth and development.

(viii) To make a proper utilisation of various house hold assets.

(ix) To perform the physical work of home making.

(x) To make best use of the technical knowledge and information for personal and professional use.

For Home Science education to be meaningful, it should be cooperatively planned, executed and evaluated.

In this regard, Secondary Education Commission, 1952, says, "An educated girl who can run her home smoothly and efficiently contributes to the happiness and the well being of her family or to raising the social standards in her country."

QUESTIONS

1. Define Home Science, "The scope of Home Science is bleak in our country." Comment on the statement.

2. Define Home Science and briefly discuss the scope of it.

5

Department Organisation

The maintenance of high standards in college departments of Home Science and the improvements of these departments depend upon continuing evaluation. A thorough going evaluation of a department of Home Science is much more complex and difficult task. The criteria of excellence are very much, their application involves the collection of a variety of evidence, and the standards are more difficult to objectify. The organisers should undertake the responsibility for developing materials and procedures for making evaluation more valid.

Basic Principles

To start a department, principles which are generally accepted as those to be used in planning a department, are given as :

1. The department should provide facilities for teaching in all areas of family living; family meals, food storage and preservation, child development and family relations, clothing construction, and care, home improvements, home care of the sick, housekeeping, home laundry, management of a household.

2. Rooms should be so located in a school that they are easily accessible for use and for delivery of supplies and removal of wastes.

3. Rooms should be so planned and arranged that they can serve all groups which will use them.

4. Provision should be made for flexibility in arrangement of movable equipment and furnishings so that multiple use is easy.

5. Furnishings should be homelike as possible.

6. Equipment and furnishings should be comparable to those of the majority of homes in the community.

7. Size of rooms and amount of equipment should be adequate for the number of pupils who use them at any one time.

8. Equipment should be varied in kind so that pupils may have experience in working with different types.

9. All furnishings and equipment should be durable to withstand constant use by many people.

10. Heights of working surfaces, chairs and tables should be suitable for the heights of pupils who are to use them.

11. Adequate ventilation and light should be there.

12. Rooms should be provided with adequate safety devices.

13. Storage space should be suited to and adequate for all of the materials and equipments needed in teaching the various areas of home making and for the care of pupil's personal belongings.

14. Floors should be of such material that they are easy to keep clean and easy to stand on.

The above principles apply when remodeling a department as well as when planning a new one.

Usually, a limited amount of money is available. In planning for the expenditure of that money, first consider those articles which are essential, second those which would be nice to have and last, those which would be luxuries.

The **Organisation**

The space, furnishings and equipments provided for a Home Science department should be related to the programme offered. The most common needs are for classrooms, laboratory facilities and teaching aids in home management, housing, house furnishings and household equipment, child development, personal and family relations, textiles, clothing, nutrition, foods and family health. The Home Science environment should exemplify the good selection, use and care of physical facilities adapted to the school situation and; the economic level of family living with which a particular department is most concerned.

The amount of space needed by a department depends upon its programme, plans for expansion and the number of students enrolled or desiring to enroll in Home Science subject. A location connected for students and reasonably close to other departments in which many Home Science students have classes is desirable. Space designed for flexibility of use best serves the multiple and varying needs of the department.

Furnishings and Equipments: The furnishings and equipments should be adequate in kind and amount for the programme. They should also be safe, hygenic, economical, well cared for and in good condition. The arrangement and furnishings should exemplify good practices in management. Worn-out and outmoded furniture and equipment should be rebuilt or replaced. Plans for future purchases of furnishings and equipments should be suitable and achievable.

Teaching Aids: A wide variety of teaching aids is needed in all areas of Home Science. Such teaching aids include books, bulletins, periodicals and other printed materials; charts and records; pictures, slides, films, projectors and cameras; and community facilities brought to the classroom; or used through field trips. Transportation for field trips should be arranged by the department.

Location of the Department: A department on the first floor of the main building which has two or more stories has advantage. It is convenient for bringing in supplies and disposing of waste materials. Rising odours of cooking food are often annoying throughout the upper floors. A department located on the second or top floor is assured of better light and air. The classes are disturbed less by the passing of other classes, and since the Home Science classes usually meet for longer periods and are smaller in size, there are fewer students to go up and down stairs.

For each department of Home Science, the following considerations should be there :

Family Living and Home Management: Laboratory facilities for home management and family living experiences should include a living unit that approximates the conditions and facilities of a well-managed home at a suitable economic level and space, furnishings and equipments should be sufficient for the laboratory. The furnishings and equipments should be of good quality and construction, economical in price and artistic in arrangement, colour, line and design.

Child Development: A good Home Science department provides facilities for studying the all-round development of children. These facilities may include :

(i) A specially planned child development laboratory, in or outside the department.

(ii) Storage space for toys, books and other supplies for teaching child development.

(iii) Supplies needed for teaching the care of babies-bathing, feeding and dressing.

Foods and Nutrition: A good Home Science department provides adequate facilities and space for the study of nutrition, food selection and purchase, food preparation and preservation and meal planning and service, with emphasis on high standards and efficient management. The food laboratories should be roomy, orderly, attractive and well lighted and ventilated, with convenient outlets for electrical and/or gas equipment and hot and cold water.

The needs to be met in Foods and Nutrition laboratory include general equipments like refrigerators, gas stoves, sinks, tables, stools and chairs, modern and of good material, workmanship and design, work areas satisfactory in size, arrangement and height, bulletin boards and blackboards; teaching aids like charts and reference materials, pictures, films and film strips, books, bulletins and pamphlets. Other needs include adequate, convenient and suitable space for receiving, storing and dispensing food, storage space for cleaning supplies and equipment, such student materials like books, practical copies and overalls etc. A conveniently located service area should be provided for the use of service, personnel and for sorting laundry, storing linens and for storing trolleys when not in use.

Textiles and Clothing: A good Home Science department provides adequate facilities for studying the selection, use and care of textile materials for clothing and the home, and for clothing construction. Textile laboratory should be roomy, attractive, orderly and well-lighted and ventilated, storage facilities that are adequate, convenient, suitable, properly used, and orderly for student's materials, for hanging unfinished and finished garments, and for illustrative materials, equipment and supplies.

The general equipments needed for textiles and clothing include comfortable chairs and tables which are of good materials, workmanship and design and which promote good posture, bulletin boards, blackboards; equipments for teaching the physical and chemical properties of textiles, including microscopes and chemical and physical testing equipments and supplies; mirrors, sewing machines, irons, ironing boards and other pressing equipments. All equipments should be arranged for convenience, safety and good management practices.

Teaching aids are of special value in this area. The important materials are textile and merchandising publications; household linens, rugs, draperies, wall hangings and upholstery materials used in Home Science department, nursery school and the Home Management units; textiles for teaching the selection and care of fabrics and clothing, including laundry equipment.

Certain problems common to the department as a whole require planning. The location of blackboards, bulletin boards and display cases in relation to unableness is important. The amount of light needed, the number and location of wall outlets for electrical conveniences, cross ventilation in a food's laboratory, adequate water supply, garbage disposal all present problems. Colours most satisfactory for wall finishes are cream, buff, gray, green-gray. A flat finish reflects less light than an enamel one. Woodwork in the foods laboratory may be finished in washable paints. Floors should be easy to clean.

The department, its furnishings and equipments should be adequate in amount and kind for direct-teaching purposes. In addition they should be selected for their value as illustrative material in a wide range of teaching situations. Money available, size of classes and the nature of the instruction to be given have effect on the provision for space and equipment. Storage is important. If the space provided is small due to lack of funds, small classes at the time, or a programme limited in scope, plans for enlargement should be included. Much of the criticism regarding the space and equipment demanded for Home Science department would be eliminated if the whole set-up was thought through in relation to its greatest usefulness as a teaching medium.

Size of the Laboratory	= 35′ x 30′
Size of Each Table	= 50" x 40"
Size of Sink	= 21" x 16"
Size of Centre Slab	= 21′ x 5′
Size of Teacher's Room	= 15′ x 10′
Size of Store Room	= 15′ x 10′
Width of Side Slab	= 2′
Size of Stools	= 1′ x 1′

Clothing and Textiles Laboratory

Size of the Laboratory = 35' x 30'

I = Bulletin Board

II = Bulletin Board

III = Black Board

IV = Dressing Table

V = Teacher's Table with Storage Space

VI = Table with felt tops with Storage Space

VII = Slab

VIII = Sink

IX = Ironing Board

X = Cloth Dryer

XI = Washing Machine

XII = Show case with Storage Space at the lower side

XIII = Show case with Storage Space at the lower side

Home Management Laboratory

Size of the Laboratory = 25' x 20'

I = Beds

II = Sofa

III = Centre Table

IV = Book Shelves

V = Steel Cabinet

VI = Peg Table

VII = Love Seats

IX = Study Table

X = Peg Table with Flower Vase

Library and Library Material

In evaluating the library in relation to Home Science department and in planning improvements, attention should be given on the basis for selecting library materials, the budget, reading rooms and space, the adequacy of library materials, accessibility of materials and use by students and staff.

Basis of Selecting Library Material: A good library basis its selection of reading materials in Home Science and supporting fields upon the philosophy and objectives of the Home Science programme and the curricula and special courses offered. These materials include basic text books, bulletins, pamphlets and periodicals, both general and technical for students and faculty use. A good library selects books by many different authors and keeps a good balance of materials in the different phases of Home Science and between the general courses and curricula. Recent publications should be preferred.

In the selection of books Home Science staff, staff of supporting fields in this area, library staff should provide help.

Budget for Library Material: Important factors in building up a library are the adequacy of funds in relation to departmental needs, the extent to which funds are used, the time of year in which funds are available and used and the ratio of library expenditure for each student in home economics to the average per capita expenditure of the institution.

Reading Rooms and Reading Space: The number and location of reading rooms should be adequate for the total number of students and convenient for Home Science students. Reading rooms and reading space should be well-lighted and quiet and should have comfortable chairs and satisfactory facilities for note taking. Library facilities should be extended to Home Science laboratories and classrooms. The department should provide a reading room or space for technical reading and general reading.

Adequacy of Library Material: The library should have the basic reading and reference materials necessary for successful teaching and learning in education for home and family life, for the cultural and inspirational reading; books and technical journals for faculty use. Library materials should be kept upto date and should be expanded as need arises. Adequate provision should be made for informing faculty members of new books and other publications. A systematic plan for discarding outdated material should be there.

The number of copies of any publication to be purchased should be in proportion to its importance for the department, its probable permanence of value and the size of the group that will use it at any one time. Reading materials should be readily accessible and a convenient and comfortable place for using them should be provided.

Accessibility of Materials: The library should be open for the convenience of students through the lunch hour, late afternoons, evenings and Saturdays. Periodicals and some books in all areas of Home Science should be on open shelves. The use of library facilities should be made as easy as possible and student schedules should be planned to allow time for reading.

Use of Library and Library Materials: Reference lists for all courses should be supplied regularly to the library. The use of reserve material should be checked, and only those materials that are used sufficiently by students to justify special handling should be kept on reserve. Reading lists should indicate clearly and correctly where books are located and the call numbers for securing them. Students should be prepared to use the library for both class preparation and leisure reading and to make use of library materials in the laboratories. The extent to which teachers use library facilities influences student's use of the library.

All the books should be classified. There can be arrangement for taking the books for class use from the general library for the period of specific study. Some books needed for the units may be used so little during class time that they should remain in the general library for use during study periods. Easy accessibility to books has a great advantage. Some libraries provide special open shelves for different classes, and books not needed in the classroom are requisitioned by the teacher to put on that shelf for a certain unit and are accessible to the pupils for use in the library without going to the call desk.

Government Printed Material: Various government agencies prepare materials on the different aspects of home living. Such material is valuable, up-to-date at the time published and available free or at a nominal cost. Teachers should keep in touch with these sources, counting on them for much current information. Such agencies usually have mailing lists sending out announcements of materials.

Magazines: Several magazines serve the needs of the homemaker. Most newspapers, either during the week or on Sunday, carry some household information. Magazines supply information about styles, new fabrics, and colour combinations each season. They present seasonal menus, recipes and housekeeping suggestions. Many have specialists in their staff who maintain the testing services and report the results of their findings. All printed materials should be evaluated as to completeness, point of view expressed and reliability.

Films: Educational films are available. Some of these teach a specific lesson; sanitary and unsanitary home conditions, the life of the silk worm and making of silk fabric. Commercial films may have features of special value; the dress, furniture and house arrangements in some historical films are especially interesting and instructive.

Equipments for a Home Science Laboratory

Food Laboratory

1.	Steel Thalis	6
2.	Steel full size plates	12
3.	Steel Quarter plates	12
4.	Steel katoris	2 dozen
5.	Tablespoons	2 dozen
6.	Tea spoons	2 dozens
7.	Serving spoons	12
8.	Kadachi	6
9.	Kadahi (Aluminium/Steel)	6
10.	Patila (Aluminium/Steel)	6

11.	Masala boxes	6
12.	Iron Tawa	6
13.	Shallow frying pans	3
14.	Sauce pans	3
15.	Knives (Iron)	6.
16.	Rolling boards and pins	6
17.	Wooden spoons	6
18.	Tea Strainers	6
19.	Big Strainers	6
20.	Steel tongs	6
21.	Steel Dongas	6
22.	Steel Glass	12
23.	Pressure Cookers	6
24.	Mixer-cum-blender	2
25.	Egg beaters	3
26.	Mashers	3
27.	Lemon squeezers	3
28.	Plastic bowls (Medium size)	6
29.	Ovens	3
30.	Baking dishes (different sizes and shapes)	6
31.	Baking trays	6
32.	Glass bottles	6
33.	Dinner plates (full)	12

34.	Dinner plates (quarter)	12
35.	Juice glasses	12
36.	Water glasses	12
37.	Dinner katories	12
38.	Cutlery sets	2
39.	Flour sievers	2
40.	Vegetable peelers	2
41.	Graters	6
42.	Food covers (all sizes)	12
43.	Steel containers (1 kg size)	12
44.	Plastic containers (different size)	12
45.	Balance	1
46.	Measuring spoons	6 sets
47.	Measuring cups	6
48.	Measuring glasses	6
49.	Dustbins	2
50.	Napkins	12
51.	Table mats	6
52.	Table covers	2
53.	Soap cases	6
54.	Tomato cutter	1
55.	Butter case	2
56.	Jelly Moulds	3

57.	Stools	According to number of students
58.	Cooking gas stoves	6
59.	Micro oven	1
60.	Cooking range	1
61.	Refrigerator	1
62.	Idli maker	2
63.	Steamers	2
64.	Toasters	2
65.	Tongs	6
66.	Palta	6
67.	Beaters	6
68.	Parat	6
69.	Chimta	6
70.	Jugs	6
71.	Trays (different sizes)	6
72.	Tray cloth	6

Home Management Laboratory

1.	Table mats	6
2.	Table covers	2
3.	Cutlery sets	2
4.	Dinner sets	2
5.	Flower vases (different sizes and metals)	12

6.	Stem holders (different sizes and shapes)	12
7.	Trolley	1
8.	Tools for cleaning (brushes, brooms, dusters)	6
9.	Mugs	6
10.	Bed	1
11.	Bedsheets	4
12.	Mattress	1
13.	Pillows	2
14.	Various brushes	12
15.	Buckets	6
16.	Vacuum cleaner	1
17.	Napkins	2 dozen
18.	Dustbin	2

Nursery Laboratory

1.	Durries	2
2.	Toys of different kinds	
3.	Blocks of different shapes and colours	
4.	Different games	
5.	Dinner set of small size	1
6.	Bulletin board	2
7.	Small chairs and tables	

8.	Dustbins	2
9.	Buckets	6
10.	Mugs	6

Tailoring-cum-Laundry Laboratory

1.	Sewing machines	6
2.	Irons	3
3.	Scissors	3
4.	Measuring tapes	3
5.	Bobbin cases	6
6.	Ironing boards	3
7.	Sleeve boards	3
8.	Pin cushions + pins	6
9.	Tables with felt top 36" x 48" x 30′	6
10.	Stools 20" height 14" diameter	12
11.	Chairs	6
12.	Teacher's storage cabinet	1
13.	Teacher's table	1
14.	Full-length mirror	1
15.	Washing machine	1
16.	Drying racks-portable	2
17.	Basins	6

18.	Buckets	6
19.	Mugs	6
20.	Tailoring Chalks	12
21.	Pinking Shears	1
22.	Measuring yardsticks	2
23.	Hangers	12
24.	Cloth pegs	2 dozen
25.	Suction-washer	1
26.	Scrubbers	6
27.	Containers	6
28.	Napkins	6
29.	Towels	6
30.	Tubs	6
31.	Microscope	1
32.	Soap cases	6

Buying Equipment and Furnishing

While purchasing new equipments or furnishings, the following principles should be followed :

Cost is an Important Consideration and should be considered in relation to suitability and durability. Consideration of cost does not mean buying the article which costs the least, but that one which costs the least in terms of quality for school use.

Durability under constant use is a necessary quality of school equipment and furnishings. Dining chairs which are durable for use at home may not be strong enough in the class because many students use them for longer duration. Small equipments like measuring cups, egg beaters and pans should be sturdier than is necessary in a home.

Tables should be stronger and the tops more durable. Tops must be impervious to acid and alkalie stains, resistant to heat and easy to keep clean. They should reduce noise and not be of such a hard material that dishes break easily when placed on them rather carelessly.

Sewing machine should be quiet, heavy enough to stand constant use and not so complicated that they get out of adjustment easily. Service facility should be easily available.

Furnishing should be Similar to those of Homes in the Community: Expensive table linens in a poor community are not suitable. Simple mats made by the students would be more suitable. Unpainted book shelves can be purchased and finished by the class. This can make excellent class projects.

Equipment and Furnishings should be Suitable to the Ages of Pupils: Likes and dislikes of the eighth grade differ from those of the eleventh and twelfth. These differences will show in the kind of dishes or pictures that interest them.

Height of tables, chairs, ironing boards and other working surfaces need thinking. If the rooms are used only by the junior high school children, heights can be adjusted for them. Same is required for the senior high school students. If both groups use the rooms, it becomes a problem since sinks, tables, chairs, cabinets are permanent fixtures. Small platform on rollers or low step ladders make it possible for the smaller pupils to reach high shelves. Other way is to keep the articles used by seventh and eighth grade classes on low shelves, those used by senior high school students on the higher ones.

Students should Share in Buying Equipment and Furnishings: Purchases for replacements or for additions to the department can become effective problems in consumer buying and home management. Buying efficient egg beaters, mixers, knives, best washing machine, attractive flower containers can become interesting if students participate in this affair. Students are always interested in purchasing new things for the department and through that interest the teacher can help them develop judgement in buying.

QUESTIONS

1. Suggest some inexpensive and improvised facilities for a functional class room for Home Science activities.
2. Write short note on Library reading.
3. Suppose you are appointed Head of Home Science Department in a newly started institution. How would you set up your laboratory.

6

Role of the Teacher

The successor failure of a Home Science course rests mainly with the Home Science teacher. He may be provided with all the possible facilities in terms of laboratory, apparatus and equipment. Given an ideal syllabus and sufficient time for teaching of Home Science but he is not likely to achieve success unless he is enthusiastic about his work, knows the subject and really knows how to teach Home Science. On the other hand a keen and well informed teacher who loves his subject and believes in its value will succeed inspite of difficulties and handicaps.

In this regard the Kothari Commission report (1966) says, "Of all the different factors which influence the quality of education and its contribution to national development, the quality, competence and character of teacher are undoubtedly the most significant"

Dr. S. Radha Krishan emphasises the role of teacher in the following words, "The teacher's place in society is of vital importance. He acts as the pivot for transmission of intellectual traditions and technical skills from generation to generation, and helps to keep the lamp of civilisation burning. He not only guides the individual, but also, so to say, the destiny of nation. Teachers have therefore to realise their special responsibility to the society. On the other hand it is in content on the society to pay due regard to the teaching profession and to ensure that the teacher is kept above want and given the status which will command respect from his student".

The Importance

"A teacher is more like a gardener who tends each plant, examines water and see that plant may take its own nourishment. The teacher should be a guide, helper and a friend. The teacher must study the child, must know the effect of environment on the child, and should know the laws of learning for which a study of psychology is necessary."

The teacher is an integral part of the process of education. He imparts education and teaches his students the subject matter prescribed for them. He has to perform a difficult job. If the teacher is an embodiment of right conduct in thought, word and deed, the students by their association will learn virtue and develop manly qualities.

Since the teacher is the pivot of any educational system for younger pupils so on her rests the failure or success of the systems.

The teacher is the dynamic force of the school. "There is no greater need for the cause of education today than the need for strong manly men and womanly women as teachers for the young."

The teacher is the yard-stick that measures the achievements and aspirations of a nation. The work and potentialities of a country get evaluated in through the work of a teacher. 'The people of a country are the enlarged replica of their teacher." They are the real nation-builder.

The Functions

Some of the important functions to be discharged by a teacher are as under:

(1) He is expected to bring about the successful teaching and build up understanding and motivation among the students.

(2) He is expected to study and organise the learning plans of the students and distribute the load for each student in a proper and scientific manner.

(3) The teacher is also expected to give due regard to individual differences.

(4) The teacher is also expected to create in the students the interest for the subject through proper appreciation of the achievement of the students. Through personal contact and knowledge, he can create love for the subject.

The Qualities

As in the case of other teachers, many things are expected of the teacher of Home Science. Teaching is not an easy job. A teacher has to bear in mind many factors-the children with their individual difference and objectives of the subject, the selection of suitable subject-matter, method of teaching etc. His obligations are not only confined to the class-room but also extend in many other directions.

No teacher can do a thorough good job of teaching Home Science unless he is willing to make a careful analysis of his job and be guided by that analysis in making his preparations and in conducting the work of his class.

Following qualities are expected in a good Home Science teacher:

Thorough Knowledge of the Subject: If a teacher has a thorough knowledge of his subject it gives him confidence in his teaching. If a teacher is not clear about certain facts or rules., She will be afraid lest she should be caught somewhere. Suppose a pupils asks a question and the teacher is not able to give a satisfactory answer. She will fail to exercise her influence on the students. They will no longer listen to her attentively. She may have some problems of indiscipline as well.

Knowledge of Methods: Only having good knowledge of Home Science is not sufficient. The teacher should be able to communicate his knowledge to the pupils. For that, teacher must be well conversant with the various methods of teaching the subject. She should have professional training. She must know the latest methods and techniques of teaching. As far as possible, the teacher should be trained, particularly in case of secondary school teachers.

There are two equally important aspects of any true profession, viz., significant knowledge and effective technique. One can not be efficiently professional if there is any serious weakness in either of the two.

In the beginning of his carrier the teacher will need to spend most of his time in improving his knowledge of teaching field and her technique of teaching.

Interest in the Subject: The Home Science teacher must have a love for his subject. Such a love and interest in subject would help him to create a similar love and interest for Home Science in her students.

Love for the Students: A teacher must love his students. Unless the teacher likes them, they will not like him. Like or dislike is reciprocal process. If the students do not like the teacher, the students will not like his subject. So the first essential before a teacher is to establish rapport with the students. She should understand them, their abilities, interests, achievement etc.

Impressive Personality: The teacher should process an impressive personality. She should have a thorough command on the subject and should be able to present it in such a manner that students grasp what she says or does in the class-room.

The teacher should keep himself properly dressed and should possess presentable physical features. There should be an aptitude of sobriety and seriousness in the teacher. This helps in discipline. The teacher should have healthy qualities. Her behaviour should serve as an ideal to the students.

Knowledge of Educational Psychology: The teacher mast have knowledge of child psychology. It is then possible for her to know the psycho-physical requirements of her students and organise her teaching accordingly.

Capacity to Inspire Confidence in Students: The teacher of Home Science should have the capacity to inspire confidence in her students. This can be done only by example and devotion to duty and certain other qualities. If the teacher can inspire confidence in her students, she can very safely carry them along with herself.

Proper Habits and Attitudes: A good Home Science teacher is expected to possess good habits like patience, confidence, hard work, initiative etc. She is expected to have rational and Heuristic attitude. She is expected to possess a strong will power and a power of concentration. She is also expected to possess neat and systematic habit of work. She is expected to possess qualities of cooperation and sympathy.

Awareness of Aims: The teacher must be clear about the aims and objectives of teaching of Home Science at various stages. Such a knowledge helps him in carrying out his job thoroughly.

Originality: The quality of originality is a must for every teacher and so is the case with a Home Science teacher. This helps the teacher to devise ways and means for imparting knowledge effectively and properly. Her approach should be original and he should not depend on any particular book-text or help book.

Knowledge of Application of Home Science: The teacher should have a good knowledge of the application of Home Science to other subjects, vocations, real life etc. Such a knowledge is quite helpful in making the teaching meaningful and interesting.

Organising Ability: A good teacher is expected to be a good organiser. She is required to organise her teaching work and other co-curricular activities such as activities of Home Science club, library etc. She has also to organise tests etc.

Capacity of Analysis and Comprehensive Description: While teaching a subject a teacher is required to give even minute details to explain things to his students. For giving such details teacher should possess the capacity of analysis. A Home Science teacher should also possess skills such as computational skill, drawing and sketching skill, problem solving skill etc.

Up-to-date Knowledge of the Subject: A teacher must keep his knowledge up to date. She should study various journals and other useful books on the subject. She should attend refresher courses, work shops, seminars etc. on the subject. She may do professional research work. She may join various Home Science Organisation, visit good schools and hold discussions with requited teachers of the subject.

Capacity to Prove Things More by Action than by Words: "Practice is better than precept". This is true for a Home Science teacher like any other teacher. The teacher has to prove things by example and not by words. If she can do that, she is sure to influence her students and so she will be able to make them interested in her subject.

Studiousness: The teacher is expected to be studious. Studiousness is essential to keep one's knowledge up-to-date.

Presence of Mind: Presence of mind is the basic requirement of any teacher. Unless she possess this quality she will not be able to solve the difficulties that beset her path in the teaching of her subject in the classroom.

Aesthetic and Artistic Outlook: Such an outlook helps the teacher in presenting things in proper perspective in an attractive manner.

Continuing Professional Development

A Home Science teacher is expected to possess certain academic qualification as also certain professional qualifications.

As regards the academic qualifications it is usually a pass in matriculation/senior secondary examination for becoming a Home Science teacher in a primary school. A pass in B.Sc. examination for being a Home Science teacher in a middle or high school and pass in M. Sc. examination in the subject for becoming a teacher to teach the subject in a senior secondary school (grade 11 and 12).

In addition to the minimum academic qualification any one who wishes to be appointed a teacher in Home Science has to undergo a teachers training course. For this purpose, a person for appointment as a teacher in primary school has to undergo 1 or 2 years Junior Basic Training (J.B.T.) course and for appointment in high and higher secondary school the graduate or post-graduate teacher has to be under a B.T. or B. Ed. course. This professional training is all the more important these days when new techniques of teaching, evaluation etc. are being introduced. Trained Home Science teachers also require the stimulus of a refresher course to keep himself informed about the latest methods of teaching and to refresh his knowledge of Home Science. Such a refresher course also provides her with an opportunity to see some of the latest books and apparatus concerning Home Science teaching and to obtain instructions in arts and scientific hobbies. During such refresher course she also gets practical training in the organisation of Home Science clubs, fairs, etc. For keeping herself in touch with latest in Home Science the teacher may visit some nearby schools where Home Science is taught by new methods. She can also take up the membership of a good library or good science association. She can think of other such institutions and industrial houses nearby from where he can get the latest knowledge of Home Science. All this is quite essential because a good teacher must always keep herself informed of the latest development in the field. This aspect of a teacher has been brought out in the following words by Dr. Rabinder Nath Tagore, "A teacher can never teach unless he is still learning himself. A lamp can not light another lamp unless it continues to burn its own flame".

Continuing professional development refers to an attempt to increase the competency of present Home Science teacher through seminars, workshops, conference, study groups, courses, lectures etc. For this purpose any formed or informed programme can be undertaken but such a programme should contribute to the professional growth of the teacher who are already in service. Some of the activities that could be undertaken are as follows:

(i) Providing opportunities to observe and participate in outstanding educational programmes.

(ii) Conducting parent-teacher meetings. During such meeting many an educational problem such as "Post-school adjustability of the pupils" can be discussed and sorted out.

(iii) Organising seminars and workshops so as to demonstrate modern teaching devices. It is desirable to demonstrate in service teachers such modern teaching devices as 'term teaching', 'micro-teaching', 'open space' etc.

Term Teaching is a process whereby teachers can cooperate in planning, teaching evaluating and observing the learning environment. Such a term approach provides for "a teacher-teacher visibility, interaction, sharing and thus provides the potential for collaborative supervision".

Micro-Teaching may be considered as, "bring down a teaching situation in terms of time, methodology and content." It provides an opportunity for teachers and supervisors to try out teaching ideas without risk of an actual situation.

Open Space is a way that helps in promoting "Cooperative teaching and learning, availability of specialised resources, differentiated staffing, independent study and use of multi media." It frees the teacher to see each other's work to collaborate, to evaluate each other and to describe each other.

(iv) To help the teachers in acquiring special skills such as curriculum development, instructional improvement, demonstration, research and dissemination etc.

(v) To facilitate teachers to go to some other schools and to see for themselves other teachers and instructors at work.

(vi) Faculty meetings are quite helpful in improving the quality of staff and an opportunity for cooperative thinking. Such meetings also help to know the total school.

(vii) Promotion of creative teaching. "Creativeness is a conscious state of experimentation" This experimentation has three phases viz., planning, testing and revising. A clear sense of direction be provided by the supervisor for promoting creativeness in teachers.

(viii) To provide opportunities to teachers for the conduct of action research in their respective class-rooms.

(ix) To arrange extension courses to provide opportunities to in-service teachers for active participation in them.

Teacher's Diary

Just like other teachers a Home Science teacher should also keep a diary. In this diary, the record of the syllabus drawn up by the Home Science teacher be maintained. It should clearly indicate the particulars of quarterly and weekly distribution of work. A copy of time-table be also kept in diary. The time-table should clearly show the distribution of available time for: (i) class room and laboratory work, (ii) Project and other allied activities (iii) Outdoor activities (excursions, visits etc.).

A record of daily work be entered in the diary regularly and it should be dated. In keeping this daily record teacher should clearly mention the details of lecture-cum-demonstration work, individual experimental work, slides etc to be shown and any such other details. He should also enter in his diary: (i) those parts of the proposed work that have been accomplished, (ii) those parts of the proposed work that could not be accomplished, (iii) any other extra work that has been attempted.

The diary should also show details of written works and questions set. Entries of any comments on assignments and practical work must also find a place in teacher's diary.

If possible teacher should also mention the mistakes that were committed by a majority of students. Such as entry will be helpful to the teacher and he can explain these mistakes to the class.

The results of the class tests and house examinations must also be recorded in the teacher's diary. A Home Science teacher can also keep a record of various chemicals, apparatus etc. ordered, for his reference, in his diary. Such a record will be quite useful for him when he is placing the orders at the beginning of the year.

Student's Note-Books

It is expected of each student to have three note-books, one of these should be practical note-book, the remaining two are ordinary note-books, one of these two be used for taking notes and copying black-board summaries and the other for assignments. It would be much convenient if all the students have some type of practical note-books and the two note-books to be used for taking notes and for assignment purposes are of different colours. Teacher should emphasise that all note-books must be kept clean and maintained properly. It would be useful if right hand page is used for writing and left-hand page is left blank for corrections, diagrams and, calculations. This blank page can also be used for further notes from textbooks, library books etc.

Record of individual practical work should be kept in practical notebook. The observation should always be directly recorded in fair practical note-book.

For practical class, some teachers use printed note-books but such note-books be avoided in higher classes.

Pupils' Home Task

The teacher should give home work to the students and check their notebooks regularly and should also maintain a record of it. In Home Science home work consists of preparatory work of assignment set or of learning the work covered in demonstration lesson or to write answers to one or two questions on the topic of demonstration. Occasionally keeping in view the availability of time teacher may ask her students to read from some popular Home Science books, magazines etc. and even ask them to write something on what they have read.

The correction of note books and the marking of errors in them takes a lot of teachers free time but it is useless to assign work to student if the teacher does not find time to mark and correct their work. The efforts be made to reduce this burden to the minimum. For this teacher may use some selected codes of symbols to make corrections and ask the students to make corrections themselves.

While making correction, all efforts be made by the teacher to point out mistakes in style and language. He should encourage the students to use a simple and straight forward language.

Inspection of Department

The teacher should always be prepared for the inspection of her department. Such an inspection is quite essential for the evaluation of whole educative process and thus improves the teaching of Home Science.

The inspection must be carried out at least once a year. It should be carried out by a team which must include at least one expert in Home Science. While carrying out inspection the team should pay special attention to the following points.

Teacher: The inspection team should see that the Home Science teacher possess the required academic and professional qualifications. The team should also pay attention to his teaching method. The individuality of teacher's method should be respected and the team if it so feels may suggest an alternative method but it should not be insisted upon. The inspection team should see that the science teacher practice proper correlation and coordination of science with other science subjects and also with other school subjects and environment.

Scheme of Work: Inspection term should see that the teacher prepares a quarterly and weekly scheme and such a scheme as shown in his diary is followed by him.

Teacher's Diary: The inspection team should see if the science teacher is maintaining his diary properly. Whether or not is he keeping a daily record of work done both in theory and practical, homework assigned etc. Has he noted down his timetable in diary? Is he having a good time-table? Is he having enough time for practicals? Is he teaching some other subjects? etc.

Text Books and Library Books: Are the students using approved and standard text books? What type of books are available in library? Are the students using library books?

Laboratory and Equipment: The inspection term should see that adequate space and apparatus etc. are available in school. In the laboratory, there is provision for the proper storage of the apparatus, equipment, chemicals etc. Inspection team must make a report about the upkeep and tidyness of the laboratory. While making remarks about laboratory the following points be clearly mentioned:

(a) Were the pictures, charts, models etc. properly displayed in the laboratory?

(b) Did the arrangement exist in the laboratory for supply of water, disposal of waste water, first-aid box etc.?

Stock Registers: Maintenance of stock registers is one of the duties of Home Science teacher and inspection team is expected to see that various stock registers are being maintained properly, accurately and regularly. It would not be improper if the inspection team carries out the physical verification of some items and find out for themselves if the actual stock agrees with the balance shown in the stock register. The checking of stock register includes the checking of requirement register and the preparation of indents etc.

Class Work and Home Work of Students: It can easily be seen from the note-books maintained by the students. The inspection team should satisfy itself that the amount of written work done by the students is sufficient. Practical note-books and assignments have been checked properly and regularly by the teacher and the mistakes have been pointed out to the students.

Home Science Library and Home Science Museum: The importance of library and museum of teaching of Home Science is given elsewhere in the book. The inspection team while carrying out the inspection of Home Science department in a school should find if a library and museum of the department are of some good standard? Is the school library being used properly by the students? Are there arrangements for regular issue and return of books from Home Science library? What method is used by Home Science teacher to satisfy himself that his students regularly devote some time to the study of library books?

Extra-curricular Activities: The existence of Home Science club in a school provides an opportunity for carrying out extracurricular activities. Inspection team should report whether a Home Science club exist? What are the activities of Home Science club? How many tours excursions etc. have been arranged? How many of such excursions, tours were arranged to visit places of scientific interest? Has the school arranged any science fair during the year? How may films/slides shows were arranged during the year? What steps were taken to encourage students to prepare home-made apparatus? Have the students contributed any good charts/ models during the year? Have any debate/declamation/ paper reading contest/quiz contest etc. arranged?

The inspection team should also ask for the record of all such activities carried out by the school during the year. .

In addition to carrying out the inspection, the inspection team is expected to give some constructive suggestion to the Home Science master for all the activities for making improvement in Home Science teaching in schools. Such suggestion should not be forced on Home Science teacher and only those of these suggestions be implemented by the Home Science teacher which are likely to bring about a qualitative change in Home Science teaching.

QUESTIONS

1. What is the importance of teachers ?
2. What is the significance of teacher's diary ?

7

Teaching Methods

For teacher of every subject, method is important. Method is nothing but a scientific way of presenting the subject keeping in view psychological and physical requirements of the children.

For an effective learning of any subject the method has to be as good as the content. It is through method only that it is possible to make a subject interesting and useful. Without a method, teaching would be hard. The arrangement of the subject and its presentation is very important for successful teaching.

Method of teaching differs from stage to stage and from age to age group. The method to be adopted depends upon many factors which include the environment and the familiar situations or experiences that are to be correlated effectively. While teaching a set of pupils with varying interests, aptitudes one has to be aware of the psychological basis of teaching learning process.

The term 'method' can be thought of as the most effective and economic way of learning to take place among students. Communication of ideas and development of concept in a precise manner based on a logical development of subject is the most important prerequisite in teaching a subject.

Teaching is thus the most difficult task and every body is not fit to be a teacher. Some persons may have a 'flair' for teaching and such persons have the ability to awaken interest and arrest the attention of the students. Some others who are not so fortunate can improve their teaching through practice if they are fully acquainted with various methods of teaching. In order to make the children learn more effectively the teacher has to adopt the right method of teaching. For choosing right methods for a given situation, the teacher must be familiar with different methods of teaching. In this chapter an effort will be made to discuss some common methods used for teaching of Home Science.

Principle of Good Teaching

If the teaching of Home Science is to attain its highest degree of efficiency, the teachers must be thoroughly trained in the materials of instructions in the field of Home Science and must also possess a broad understanding of all the phases of methods of teaching Home Science and should thus be aware of the following principles of good method.

(i) The teacher should be quite clear about the objective to be achieved and should make all efforts to avoid all the ambiguities.

(ii) Teacher should be careful to see that there is a logical sequence in all his explanations.

(iii) Teacher should be careful to use only a simple and suitable language that could be easily comprehended by his students. To put an emphasis on certain points she should make an effective use of her voice and manners.

(iv) Important point be written on the black-board.

(v) Teacher should adopt a method that encourages the initiative of the students.

(vi) All efforts be made to avoid memorisation and teaching through purposeful, realistic and concrete way should be followed.

(vii) All the facts selected for presentation should be dealt with in full.

(viii) All out efforts be made to create interest among the pupils.

(ix) Maximum use be made of pictures, charts and models.

(x) The teacher must take into consideration the individual difference while teaching in the class.

(xi) Teacher should follow a variety of methods.

Various Methods

Many a method is available that could be successfully used for the teaching of Home Science. These methods of teaching have been broadly classified as :

1. Teacher-centred Methods, and

2. Pupil-centred Methods.

Teacher-centred Methods

(a) Discussion method,

(b) Laboratory method,

(c) Demonstration method, and

(d) Demonstration-cum-discussion method.

Pupil-centred Methods

(a) Field trip method,

(b) Problem solving method,

(c) Project method,

(d) Group work,

(e) Assignment method, and

(f) Role playing.

These methods are described in some details in the following pages.

Discussion Method

This method is found quite suitable for those topics in Home Science which can not be easily explained by demonstration or other such techniques. In this method, there is sufficient scope for free and natural participation of the pupils. This is an elucidation method. This method may be helpful to collect information on various topics such as food fads and fallacies, marriage, customs, embroidery designs etc. The material of study is collected by the students and the teacher and then all the points are arranged in a logical sequence. While teaching by this method class and group discussion can be made use of and for such a discussion pupils may be divided into small groups, each group having its own leader. While discussing, the teacher and pupils must appreciate each other's point of view and should try to convince each other of the validity of that view point.

This method is one of the oldest methods of teaching and has many an advantage. Some of the advantages on this method are as under:

(i) It helps a lot to know about the background of the child.

(ii) It allows a better participation of pupils.

(iii) It helps to make class room teaching more lively, active and interesting.

(iv) It helps to develop qualities of leadership in the pupils.

(v) It stimulates mental activity.

(vi) It develops fluency in speaking.

(vii) It clarifies ideas and helps in the process of thinking.

(viii) It trains in the presentation of one's ideas and facts.

This method is used for teaching of Home Science. It can be used either exclusively or in combination with other methods.

Following points if kept in view help make the discussion successful:

(i) The topics for discussion should be of common interest of students.

(ii) Teacher should establish a favourable atmosphere in the class before starting the discussion.

(iii) Teacher should see that every one participates in the discussion. The whole essence of discussion is "Thinking together".

(iv) The teacher should talk to the bare minimum and also should not allow any one student to dominate the whole discussion.

(v) It is for teacher to see that the discussion remains a discussion and it does not change into a debate.

(vi) Teacher should keep a check on answers of the students and should not allow a student to go beyond the scope of a topic under discussion.

(vii) Teacher has to maintain discipline and he should see that only one student speaks at a time.

Constituents of a Discussion : The essential parts of this method are the teacher, the group leader, the group, the problem, the content and the actual process of discussion.

Role of Teacher

In a group discussion, the teacher or the group leader is expected to play an important role. It is a teacher-centred method and for organising a discussion teacher has to make a lot of preparations. Though it is a teacher centred method yet it is expected that teacher will not dominate over the entire scene. She is expected to play the role of a guide and help her pupil whenever they are in difficulty. The role of teacher in this method can be summarised as under:

(i) to introduce the subject,

(ii) to allow the group some time to warm up and to keep the discussion to the point,

(iii) to encourage every student to take an active part in discussion, and

(iv) to create proper climate for free interchange of ideas.

To facilitate discussion, the teacher should make proper use of various teaching aids such as black-board, pointer etc.

The Group : For discussion, a group is formed with a group leader. A group consists of pupils with different temperaments and it is the duty of the group leader to make full use of the talents of all the members of the group. He should see that every member of the group participates in discussion. All the members of the group should have equal right to contribute. Each student should feel the importance of her contribution to the discussion. An atmosphere of friendly cooperation should exist among the students. They should learn to respect honest differences of opinion.

The Problem : The problem for discussion be selected keeping in mind the interest of the students. It should be simple and precise. The teacher should seek the cooperation of her students in selecting the topic for discussion and the points to be discussed should be listed cooperatively with the students.

The Content : It refers to the body of the knowledge and is one of the topics prescribed in the syllabus for Home Science.

***Actual Process of Discussion* :** Following points be kept in mind when the discussion is in progress:

(i) At the time of discussion, effort be made not to ask question to a particular group unless there is somebody trying hard and determined to put her ideas any way.

(ii) When somebody speaks on a particular point others should not interfere.

(iii) The teacher should not impose her own views on others. She should be guided by democratic principles.

(iv) There should not be any deviation from discussion.

(v) It should flow from one member to another member.

(vi) Discussion must not flow from a member to the leader and the leader to another member.

(vii) All the discussions should be closed with accurate summaries.

***Evaluation* :** Each individual participating in a group discussion should evaluate whether the discussion has in any way helped to improve her knowledge and information, has brought about any changes in her attitudes and ideas and has enhanced the range of her interest in the subject.

***Techniques of Discussion* :** These are classified as:

(i) The formal group technique, and

(ii) The informal group technique.

The Formal Group Technique : In this technique the members constituting the group are either elected or nominated (e.g., senate, council or committee). Proper records of discussions are kept. This technique may be classified under various heads as under:

(a) Panel discussion,

(b) The symposium and the study circle,

(c) Debate,

(d) Buzz session,

(e) Workshop technique,

(f) Discussion 66, and

(g) Brain storming.

Panel Discussion : This type of discussion generally involves 4-6 persons who are experts in their field. A president or group leader is selected before the start of a panel discussion. The president initiates the discussion and allows others to speak in turn. The audience joins in the discussion by way of asking questions. The experts talk on different aspects of the problem. In this type of discussion long speeches, arguments or debates are not allowed. The basic purpose of a panel discussion is to get different facts from different angles, stimulate thinking, to lay a basis for wide participation.

At the end of the panel discussion the president summarises the panel discussion and brings out the important points emphasized.

A variation of 'Panel discussion' is "opposite panel". In "opposite panel" the class is divided into two groups, facing each other. One group asks question and the other answers. The groups are then reversed after some time or in the next chance.

Important Steps in Panel Discussion

(i) Selection of the topic. The topic after selection be put in the form of questions.

(ii) Selection of the members. The members of a group for panel discussion be selected with care. While selecting the members for a group various qualities of the pupil such as voice, manner of speaking, willingness to share ideas etc. be given due consideration.

(iii) Preparation. For any meaningful discussion it is essential that members are well conversant with the topic and all the members should come fully prepared for discussion.

(iv) Time for discussion. For a panel discussion a minimum of one period be allotted.

(v) Seating arrangement. They may be a raised platform or a stage created for the panel personnel to sit. Semi-circular seating arrangements may also be made. The audience should be enabled to clearly see and hear the panel personnel.

Advantages of Panel Discussion

(i) It stimulates mental activity, fluency in speaking etc.,

(ii) It is very helpful in collective decision making,

(iii) It helps in development of intellectual dexterity and argumentative talents,

(iv) It inculcates tolerence, and

(v) It provides scope for identifying talented students from amongst the members of the group.

Limitation of Panel Discussion

(i) ·It is not suitable for all topics.

(ii) Some times only a few students dominate the discussion.

(iii) It may create emotional tension among students.

(iv) There is scope for unnecessary arguments.

(v) Unpleasant feelings among the members of the group may be created.

(vi) It may not remain on the track. It may go out of it.

It may be noted that this panel discussion is just one of the methods of teaching Home Science. It can achieve success only by the seminar and hard working undergraduates, capable and hard working teachers.

Symposium

In a symposium, each member of the group is expected to give his view to the audience through speeches or paper reading, as the particular aspect of a problem as a specialist. At the end a mutual discussion is allowed. The symposium may be a paper reading symposium in which case the topic to be discussed is made known in advance and the participants present their papers at the symposium. It is presided over by one of the participants and another are from amongst the participants act as stage secretary. The symposium is wound up by the speech of the president in the form of presidential remarks.

The other forms are lecture symposium and study circle.

The Debate

A debate is always organised between two groups. It is also a form of group discussion. For a debate some specific topic is selected and one group gives arguments in favour of it whereas the other group argues against it. There is a hot argument because each group tries to counter balance the arguments put forward by the other group. In case of formal debates, judges are requested to observe the arguments so as to determine the superiority of one of the groups.

Buzz Session

In this type of session (buzz meaning ringing) the class breaks off into pairs to discuss an issue. A pair changes its partner at the buzz of the bell. Each pair records suggestions made by the participants.

Brain Storming

In this technique, which is found to be more suitable for business firms, the brains of participants are stimulated to create a 'storm of ideas' and suggestions about a topic. The storm of ideas help in solving a problem. Any idea whatsoever is accepted. For the success of this it, is essential to have a person-to-person informal relationship between the teacher and the students and also amongst the students themselves. Moreover simple problem familiar to students and having a number of solutions is selected and announced by the teacher sufficiently before to enable the participants to come prepared for the discussion. It is also desirable for the teacher to be creative and efficient so that she can suggest a solution to the problem under discussion. To test the reality of a solution it is also desirable to follow up the solution.

Discussion 66

The name of this discussion emphasises the fact that in this type of discussion 6 participants meet for 6 minutes and discuss a problem. Thus each one of the six participants gets a minute in this type of discussion. Making use of this technique it is possible to collect the opinion of a large number of students in a limited time available.

Seminar Plan

It is a plan generally meant for advanced students. It may work well at the college level but may also be adopted to the seminar classes of a high school. This seminar plan aims at the development of the power of expression, co-operation in thinking and talking development or original study and to provide to students opportunities for expressing their ideas.

A problem is selected for a seminar and various solution to the problem are offered by a number of students who have investigated the problem either individually or in association with some other students. The criticism is then invited for the various solutions offered. Each solution in critically assessed by the group and in this way work of all members of the group is evaluated in a group conference.

In conducting a seminar the teacher acts as a leader of the group and exercises her control so as to keep the discussion limited to the topic. She also has to see that all the participants are allowed a chance to speak in the seminar. The benefit of a seminar is that here we discuss a number of probable solutions and such a discussion is quite useful for the participants as they can gain better understanding through mutual discussion.

Workshop Technique

The seminar may sometimes take the form of a work-shop. In a workshop, the participants decide how to evolve a programme and how to proceed. In it, more emphasis is laid on practical work than on theoretical discussion and it is on this score that it differs from seminar.

In this the group works as a whole. In it each individual contributes his mite. For convenience the bigger group may be divided into smaller groups and in that case there is provision of time and for general session of the whole group and specific session for smaller groups. In case smaller groups meet for a longer time they are called interest groups.

The members in interest groups may work on different aspects of the same problem. The report prepared by the interest group is discussed in the general session and a conclusion is arrived at in such a session. For expert guidance in some field, we can take the help of some experts in the respective fields. These experts are called resource personnel.

When a project has been executed with success the participants (students) are asked to critically evaluate the project. This evaluation may be done either individually or in groups.

Laboratory Method

For the teaching of Home Science, we have come a long way from the time when a textbook was the only equipment considered necessary. The modern teacher is becoming more and more concerned with the facilities that are needed for "learning by doing". Laboratory experiences under the supervision of a teacher provides the students with an opportunity to learn by doing with the increasing number of teaching aids, the idea developed of a Home Science laboratory. The idea of a Home Science laboratory has given rise to demands for such a laboratory on that the Home

Science department is entitled to one because better equipment is essential in teaching the Home Science. The capable educational administrator tries to get for his teacher as much equipment they need so that they have opportunity of doing good work. Material aids of instruction are essential for achieving the aims and objectives of teaching Home Science. What the values of teaching this subject do, the equipments promote. Therefore, a Home Science laboratory and the laboratory of teaching this subject has been suggested by experts.

In the laboratory method of teaching Home Science, the task of teacher is to supervise the work of the class and to correct the errors of the students.

She is also expected to give suggestions to her students and also to encourage them. Whenever a need arises to explain some vague point the teacher may ask the student to stop the laboratory work and then she should explain to them the point emphasising important phase of the work.

Giving a picture of laboratory method H. C. Hill states, "The greater part of the students will be studying and writing at their work tables. Two or three may be having a quite conference on some moot point. Others may be comparing notes or outlines of some phases of the work. One student may be busy at dictionary, haunting for explanation of some phrase or term, another may be consulting an atlas, a third may be sharpening a pencil or filing his fountain pen, a fourth may be making a map or preparing a graph, a fifth may be conferring with the teacher about some difficulty or asking for a criticism on his notes or outlines, usually one or two students will be borrowing among the volumes in the book cases or going through tables of contents or indexes to find a clue to some obscure item, now and then an idler or a dwadler will be observed. In general, however, the room is a place of quite, disorderly order, in which students are busily engaged in profitable activities of one kind or another."

In teaching of Home Science laboratory experiences have the following important values:

(i) Values of productive experiences, e.g., food preparation, clothing construction etc:

(ii) Values of experimental experiences, e.g., removal of ink stain etc.

(iii) Values of observational experiences, e.g., study of fabric, comparison of soaps etc.

Parts of a Laboratory Lesson : A laboratory lesson consists of following parts :

(i) Planning,

(ii) Work, and

(iii) Summarisation and evaluation.

Planning : In the planning period a plan is developed jointly by the teacher and the students. In this the goals are set and it contains an outline of the procedure to be followed to attain the goals. It also includes the plan of procedure to be discussed in the discussion period.

Work: During this work or doing period, the experimentation, production and observation are carried out by the students. The teacher provides them the necessary help and guidance. It is actually the period for individual teaching. During this period teacher can use her influence for developing good working habit amongst her students. She can inculcate good sanitary habits and may lay emphasis on proper postures while working. Due emphasis be placed as the safety habits and performing a work in an ordered manner with neatness and cleanliness.

Summarisation and Evaluation : During this period, an evaluation of the product obtained as also of the method of work are evaluated by teacher as also the students. This period can also be used to record generalisations and to clarify certain important principles.

The time needed for laboratory experience differ according to the requirement of situation. When some laboratory experiences are concluded only in one period, others need more, when the periods are of only 40 to 45 minute duration. Two periods are combined for one laboratory experience. As far as possible the students should try to do the laboratory work individually. Each girl should have her materials to work in the class room.

Time and management in planning are two important requirements of a laboratory lesson. Therefore, the teacher has to plan every step very carefully.

Evidence or Success. The success of laboratory lessons can be evidenced from the following observations:

(i) In the activity period, the student progresses in their work quite smoothly, working independently and co-operatively.

(ii) Students work without wasting their time and energy and share responsibility for routine work.

(iii) Throughout the work period, the interest and the attention of the students are quite encouraging.

(iv) Class evaluation of the whole activity is objective.

(v) Productive work if any, is successfully carried out.

(vi) Expected pupil development takes place.

Merits of Laboratory Method

(i) It enables the child to learn by doing.

(ii) It is based on observation and first-hand experience.

(iii) It helps to bring the teacher and taught in a closer contact.

(iv) It is more democratic.

(v) It helps to develop the ability of interpretation and observation.

Limitation of Laboratory Method

(i) It is quite mechanical.

(ii) It is quite expensive.

(iii) It is time consuming.

(iv) This method is not useful for large classes.

(v) This method requires well-equipped laboratories.

(vi) Text-books in use that can be undertaken by the students.

(vii) This method tends to become an end in itself, rather than a means to an end.

Demonstration Method

In this method of teaching certain demonstrations are used to provide information to create interest or to develop standard of work by sharing how certain things are done. The teacher may demonstrate any thing to students, e.g., threading the machine etc. The students shall try to follow it. By this method it is possible to easily impart concrete experiences to students during the course of a lesson when the teacher wants to explain certain abstract points. This method combines the instructional strategy of 'information imparting' and 'showing how. This method can be easily used to teach topics like methods of cooking, washing cloths, bathing the babies etc.

This method is based on the principle, "Truth is that which works".

Requirements of a Good Demonstration : For success of any demonstration, following points be always kept in mind:

(i) It should be planned and rehearsed by the teacher before hand.

(ii) The apparatus used for demonstration should be big enough to be seen by the whole class.

(iii) Adequate lighting arrangements be made on demonstration table and a proper background be provided.

(iv) All the pieces of apparatus be placed in order before starting the demonstration. The apparatus likely to be used should be placed on the left hand side of the table and it should be arranged in the same order in which it is likely to be used. After an apparatus is used it should be transferred to right hand side, only things relevant to the lesson to be placed on demonstration table.

(v) Before actually starting the demonstration, a clear statement about the purpose of demonstration be made to the students.

(vi) The teacher must make sure that the demonstration-cum-lecture method leads to active participation of the students in the process of learning. This he can achieve by putting well-structured questions.

(vii) The demonstration should be quick and should not appear to linger on unnecessarily.

(viii) The demonstration should be interesting so that it captures the attention of the students.

(xi) The teacher must be sure of success of the experiment to be demonstrated and for this he should release the experiment under the conditions prevailing in the class room.

(x) No complaints about inadequate and faulty apparatus be made by the teacher. In such a situation, a good teacher finds an opportunity to show his skill.

(xi) It would be much better if the teacher demonstrates those experiments which are connected with common things which are seen and handled by students,in their every day life.

(xii) There should be a correlation between the demonstrations and the sequence of experiments performed by the students in their practical classes.

(xiii) For active participation of students, the teacher may call individual student, in turn, to help him in demonstration work.

(xiv) During lecture-cum-demonstration session, teacher must act like a 'showman' and 'performer'. He should know different ways of arresting the attention of the students.

(xv) He should write, a summary of the principles arrived at because of demonstration, on the black board. The black board can also be used for drawing necessary diagrams.

How to Conduct a Demonstration Lesson? We commonly find Home Science teachers making use of demonstration method for teaching of Home Science. The conduct of a demonstration lesson is very difficult and here we will try to discuss some of the essential steps that should be followed in a demonstration lesson.

Planning and Preparation : A great care be taken by the teacher while planning and preparing his demonstration lesson. He should keep the following points in mind while preparing his lesson:

(a) subject matter,

(b) questions to be asked, and

(c) apparatus required for the experiment.

To achieve the above stated objective, the teacher should thoroughly go through the pages of the text book, relevant to the lesson. After this he should prepare his lesson plan in which he should essentially include the principles to be explained, a list of experiments to be demonstrated and the type of questions to be asked from the students. These questions be arranged in a systematic order that has to be followed in the class. Before actual demonstration, a rehearsal be conducted.

Introduction of the Lesson : As in every other subject so also in case of Home Science the lesson should start with proper motivation of the students. It is always considered more useful to introduce the lesson in a problematic way which would make students realise the importance of the topic. The usual ways in which a teacher could easily introduce his lesson is by telling some personal experience or incident, a simple and interesting experiment, a familiar anecdote or by telling a story.

A good experiment when carefully demonstrated is likely to leave an everlasting impression on the young mind of the pupil and it would set his pupils talking in school and out of it, about the interesting experiment that had been demonstrated to them in the Home Science class. This should be kept in mind not only to start the lesson but be used, on every suitable occasion, during the lesson.

Presentation : The method of presenting the subject matter is very important. A good teacher should present his lesson in an interesting manner and not in a boring way. To make the lesson interesting the teacher may not be very rigid to remain within the prescribed course rather he should make the lesson as much broad based as is possible. For widening of his lesson the teacher may think of various useful applications of the principle taught by him. He is also at liberty to take examples and illustrations from other allied branches to make his lesson interesting. Thus, every effort be made to present the matter in a lively and interesting manner and lesson should never be presented as 'dry bones' of an academic course. It is also advisable to make use of pictures, posters, diagrams, slides, films etc. in addition to experiments to illustrate the topic in hand.

Constant questions and answers should form part of every demonstration lesson. Questions and cross questions are essential for properly illuminating the topic being discussed. Questions be arranged in such a way that their answers form a complete teaching unit. Though an effort be made to encourage the students to answer a large number of questions but if students fails to answer some questions teacher should provide the answers to such questions. It is unwise to expect all the answers from the pupils and a teacher should feel satisfied if he has been able to create a desire in a student to know what he does not know.

The lesson be presented in a clear voice and the teacher should speak slowly and with correct pronunciation. He should avoid the use of any bombastic and ambiguous terms. The continuous talk is likely to lead to monotony and to avoid it experiments be well spaced throughout the lesson.

Performance of Experiments : A good observer has been described as a person who has learned to use his senses of touch, sight, smell and hearing in an intelligent and alert manner. We want children to observe what happens in experiments and to have ample opportunities to state their observations carefully. We also want them to try to explain what happens in reference to their problems, but we want to make certain. There is separation between observations and generalization and conclusions.

The following steps are generally accepted as valuable in developing and concluding Home Science experiments with the children:

1. Write the problems to be solved in simple words so that every one understands.

2. Make a list of activities that will be used to solve problems.

3. Gather material for conducting experiments.

4. Work out a format of the steps in the order of procedure so that every one knows what is to be done.

5. The teacher should always try the experiment himself to become acquainted with the equipment and procedure.

6. Record the findings in ways commensurate with the maturity level and purposes of the student.

7. Assist students in making generalisations from conclusions only after sufficient evidence and experiences.

The demonstration experiment be presented by the teacher in a model way. He should work in a tidy, clean and orderly manner while demonstrating an experiment. Some of the important points to be kept in mind while demonstrating an experiment are as under:

(i) Experiments should be simple and speedy.

(ii) The experiments must work and their results should be clear and striking.

(iii) Experiments be properly spaced throughout the lesson.

(iv) Keep some reserve apparatus on the demonstration table.

(v) Keep the demonstration apparatus intact till it has to be used again.

Black Board Summary : A summary of important results and principles be written on the black board. Use of black board should also be frequently made for drawing necessary sketches and diagrams. The black board summary should be written in neat, clean and legible way. Since black board summery is an index to a teacher's ability he should keep the following points in mind while writing on black board.

(i) Proper space be left between different letters and words.

(ii) Always start writing from left hand corner of the black board.

(iii) Start a new line when the first one has extended across the black board.

(iv) Take care not to divide the words at the end of a time.

(v) Make all efforts to keep all the paragraphs and similar signs in calculations under one another.

(vi) While drawing sketches and diagrams preferably use 'single lined' diagrams.

(vii) All the diagrams drawn on the board be properly labelled.

Supervision : Students be asked to take the complete notes of the black board summary including the sketches and diagrams drawn. Such a record will be quite helpful to the student for learning his lesson. Such a summary will prove beneficial only if it has been copied correctly from the black board and to make sure that students are copying the black board summary properly the teacher should check it by frequently going to the seats of the students.

Common Errors in a Demonstration Lesson : A summary of common errors committed while delivering a demonstration lesson is given below:

(i) The apparatus may not be ready for use.

(ii) There may not be an apparent relation between the demonstration experiment and the topic under discussion.

(iii) Black board summary is not upto the mark

(iv) Teacher may be in a hurry to arrive at generalisation without allowing sufficient time to arrive at these generalisation from facts.

(v) Teacher may some times fail to ask right type of questions.

(vi) Teacher some times may use a difficult language.

(vii) Teacher some times takes to talking more which may mar the enthusiasm of the students.

(viii) Teacher may not have allowed sufficient time for recording data etc.

(ix) Teacher has not given proper attention to supervision.

Merits of Demonstration Method : Following are the merits of this method:

(i) It is economical method as compared to purely student-centerd approaches.

(ii) It is psychological method and students take active interest is teaching learning process.

(iii) It leads students from concrete to abstract situations and thus is more psychological.

(iv) It is a suitable method if the apparatus to be handled is costly and sensitive. Such an apparatus is likely to damage if handled by students

(v) This method is safe.

(vi) In comparison to Heuristic method, project etc., it is time saving but lecture method is too speedy.

(vii) It can be used successfully for all types of stunts.

(viii) In this method such experiments which are difficult for students can be included.

(ix) This method can be used to impart manual and manipulative skills to students.

Disadvantages of Demonstration Method **:** Some of the disadvantages of this method are as under:

(i) It provides no scope for 'learning by doing' for students as students just observe what the teacher is performing. Thus, students fail to relish the joys of direct personal experience.

(ii) Since the teacher performs the experiments in his own pace, many students cannot comprehend the concept being clarified.

(iii) Since the method is not child-centred it makes no provision for individual difference. All types of students including slow learners and genius have to proceed with the same speed.

(iv) It fails to develop laboratory skills in the students. It can not work as a substitute for laboratory work by students in which they are required to handle the apparatus themselves.

(v) In this method students many a time fail to observe many finer details of apparatus because they observe it from a distance.

Conclusion : This is considered to be one of the good methods of teaching Home Science. The two main reasons for using this method of teaching for teaching of Home Science are as follows:

(i) It is easier to perform practical after a demonstration has been given by the teacher.

(ii) Practicals are less expensive than pupils individually conducting practicals.

(iii) It helps to save a lot of time.

Demonstration-cum-Discussion Method

In this method all the good points of discussion method and demonstration method are combined together. In this method the teacher performs the experiments in the class and also explains what she is doing.

This method provides an opportunity to the students to participate actively in discussion, keenly observe the apparatus used, teaching aids used, and draw inference. When taught by this method, students develop power of reasoning and observation. Following points be kept in mind for the success of this method.

(i) Before coming to the class, the teacher should plan and practice the method. She should come to the classroom full of confidence.

(ii) The aims and objectives of teaching a specific topic should be clean and distinct.

(iii) The teaching aids and other apparatus used in the class should be arranged in proper manner.

(iv) Questions should be asked so as to motivate the students.

(v) Students must be explained about the difficulties in performing experiments and the necessary precautions to be taken.

(vi) With the help of questions she should try to study the power of comprehension, reasoning and observation.

(vii) The demonstration made by the teacher along with discussion should be visible to all the students present in the classroom.

(viii) At the time of discussion necessary teaching aids must be used.

(ix) Teacher should make all possible efforts to clarify all the doubts of the students.

(x) Proper use of the black-board be made by the teacher for writing the summary of the lesson.

Demerits of Demonstration-cum-Discussion Method

(i) This method is not based on the principle of 'learning by doing'.

(ii) This method does not provide a chance of direct experience, of performing the experiments, to the students.

(iii) It is essential, for the success of this method, that the teacher fully knows the technique of handling the apparatus.

Pupil-centred Methods

Field Trips : Field trips provide the students with opportunities to have direct experience with out-of-school life. Excursions occupy an important place in the teaching of Home Science. In excursions and travels students get an opportunity to observe and see things by themselves. Truly speaking excursions are the part and parcel of observation method. Therefore educationists have laid down that excursions should form a part of the teaching of Home Science. For this pupils must go for shopping under the guidance of a teacher to know what wise marketing is.

Such trips develop appreciation and understanding of things as they really are and the way to secure information at its source. There should be a definite objective and plan for a field trip after discussion. The result of the trip will be evaluated.

Field trips provide goad opportunities to teach social-customs and help to develop personal traits of courtesy, cooperation and depend ability. Field experiences are firsthand experiences. Excursions present the object in its natural colours. These excursions also serve a useful purpose of character formation of the students so that he may not be a misfit in society. Field experiences being more meaningful allow easier transfer of leanings to the solutions of real life problems. It also allows a class to engage in those activities which are too noisy or too violent for being undertaken in class-room. In a field trip, students can also work with large scale material.

The teacher uses field trip with a definite objective. The students select the goal and the plans are carefully laid by the teacher and the students. Trips are then undertaken in accordance with the plan so prepared. After the trip the results are evaluated.

After the excursion the outdoor observation work be closely related with in-door work. The students should be encouraged to study all those things so as to strengthen their knowledge and thus encourage them to proceed from concrete to abstract.

For the success of this method it is essential that the teacher himself is very fond of excursions and is willing to arrange such excursions. Teacher should be willing to face the problems and inconveniences likely to come up during such excursions.

Before undertaking a field trip, all the necessary information should be collected beforehand and all details should be well considered. It should be planned and organised very carefully.

Role of Teacher : During a field trip, the role of teacher is that of a guide and a friend. She should have a close watch on her pupils and provide specific help and, encouragement to them whenever it is needed. She should prepare herself in such a way during field trip so that she is equipped to bring the field work to close at the optimum time. For the success of field work a teacher is expected to work along with the pupils, displaying by her example how interesting the work is.

Merits of Field Trips : The merits of field trips may be summarised as follows:

(i) The field trips give wide-experiences that are rich and meaningful and can always elicit a better response.

(ii) They always lead the child to have a total experience and in this way can influence the ideas, attitudes and values very effectively.

(iii) These give ideal natural learning situations, develop observation and keenness, knowledge learnt is concrete and everlasting. The child gets familiarised with his environment.

(iv) These give opportunities for getting training in a number of odd responsibilities such as arranging for a transport, keeping accounts, child welfare, life in hospitals, weaving and knitting factories, food craft visiting super markets and living corporate life etc.

(v) Out of school life, train the pupils in the fact of life in which they learn planning for observation.

(vi) In the present-day-society, educationists advocate to make the school community-centered school and community must come closer to educate the child in a spirit of give and take. The field trip serves as a link between these two vital agencies of education and improves the interaction.

(vii) With the help of this method, instructions can be imparted even if the school does not have necessary equipments.

(viii) It helps to make lectures interesting by combining theory and practice.

Project Method

This method lays more emphasis in learning by doing'. A project as defined by Dr. Kilpatrick is, "A whole hearted purposeful activity; proceeding in a social environment." Stevenson defines a project as, "A project is a problematic act carried to completion in its natural setting." Actually speaking the term "project" has got very wide connotation and has been taken to include any activity like dramatics, pageants, making models, drawing maps and charts, collecting pictures, preparing scrap books, going on field trips or any other constructive and experimental understanding, which enables the children to learn a significant skill or process. A project may be a brief task or it may be an inclusive undertaking.

The project is a kind of life-experience which is motivated by a strong desire to learn and teaching by the project method is based upon the use of this desire. This method is in reality a method of living. Projects related to home, school and community are very useful in teaching many topics in Home Science. For example, celebration of festivals may be undertaken, to provide an opportunity to students, to learn interior decoration, cooking, entertaining guests etc. Successful completion of a project depends upon selection, planning, execution and evaluation.

The project method is a direct outcome of the Dewey's philosophy. This is a child-centred method. More emphasis is laid, in this method, on the actual action or activity on the part of the pupils. In this method, the curriculum, the content and techniques are considered from the children's point of view.

Various Steps in a Project Method : The important steps in a project method are:

Providing a Situation. To teach by this method, the teacher must provide a situation wherein the pupils are eager to carry out a project according to their needs and interests. Generally various situations are discussed by the teacher so as to find out the interest of the pupils. In such discussion students are motivated to the situation. Difficulties likely to be faced in different plans are highlighted. Resources are taken into account and various alternatives are considered. After a careful consideration a plan in selected and it is then written down in the project book by the students under the guidance of the teacher.

Choosing the Project. The choice of the project be left to the students and the role to the teacher be limited to guidance only. Dr. Kilpatric observes, "the part of the pupil and the part of the teacher in most of school work depend largely on who does the proposing. `The most important thing is that the pupils do the proposing. However, the teacher should tactfully handle the situation and see that a project of greatest educational value is chosen.

Planning. Even during this step the teacher's role is to guide and the actual planning has to be done but the pupils. During planning, maximum participation of students be ensured. During consideration of various proposals the teacher should make clear the difficulties likely to be faced in execution of a proposal. Finally, the best possible plan be approved.

Execution. After a particular plan has been approved it is executed and the project is carried out in accordance with the plan. The teacher may assign definite duties to individual students for this purpose. Every child is expected to contribute some thing in the execution of the plan and successful completion of the project. The teacher should provided only the minimum help.

This is the longest step and the students are busy in different works assigned to them. They may be busy in collecting information, visiting various places and peoples, looking up maps, writing letters, reading the reference books, calculating prices, inquiring rates etc. Guidance for all these varied activities is to be provided by the teacher and so the task of teacher is quite difficult.

A single project may provide for a number of activities and a variety of knowledge of mathematics, of science, of history, of geography etc. The students gain different types of experiences while executing a project and so they learn a good deal incidentally.

Evaluation. After its completion, the project is critically evaluated to assess if the activities have been carried out in accordance with the plan chalked out or not. Mistake committed, if any, are noted down, things learnt are reviewed and useful experiences are recounted. The importance of this step lies in the fact that it sets the pupil's thinking about the work they have accomplished and to evaluate it in the light of the experiences gained.

Recording. This is essential for any effective learning process that a complete record of all the things learnt be kept. Such a record is generally kept in a project book. The record includes every thing about the project, i.e., the choice of the project, the discussion held, proposals accepted, duties assigned, books consulted, informations sought for, work undertaken, difficulties faced, experiences gained etc. Such a record is found quite useful and so the teacher should see that a complete record of all the project undertaken is kept by the students in their project book.

Role of the Teacher in Project Method : A teacher under the project scheme is a friend, guide and philosopher of the students. She is not to act as a dictator but a director only. She is to be a practical psychologist to understand the interest and requirements of the young children. She must possess emotional maturity and intellectual patience to guide the children. She should be tactfully to direct their activities though herself keeping in the background. Help is to be given only when it is sought for and not to be imposed upon for speedy execution of the project. She is to repose confidence and goodwill in the children. So that the children are encouraged to come forward to discuss, to propose, to plan and to take up the work.

She should help the pupils to avoid mistakes. She should also help them to observe keenly and to obtain information from many a varied source. The teacher should see that the students know and realise their responsibilities to the full. The teacher should fill the gaps, if any between the knowledge acquired by the students. The teacher should always remain alert and active and should always be in search of new sources of information for the success of the project. She must be very careful while assigning duties to the students. The duties be assigned to each individual according to her abilities and capabilities.

Merits of the Project Method

(i) It is psychological method and in it the three important laws of learning are always kept in view. These laws are: (a) law of readiness, (b) law of exercise, (c) law of effect.

(ii) It is an economical method.

(iii) It gives due importance to the dignity of labour.

(iv) In it, education is imparted according to real life situations.

(v) It trains the child for a democratic way of life.

(vi) It inculcates right social habits.

(vii) It helps the students to become more responsible and self-reliant.

(viii) It helps to develop various qualities such as independence, habits of discussion, resourcefulness, self-respect etc. in the child.

(ix) It helps to develop the power of reasoning and thinking.

(x) It is a scientific method.

Difficulties in Project Method

(i) The selection of right project is very essential.

(ii) It is quite lengthy, time consuming and expensive method.

(iii) In this method there is a chance that some students may shirk work.

(iv) Since each student has to perform certain specified duties for the completion of the project, the learning will not be uniform.

(v) The teaching is haphazard and discontinuous.

Outstanding Features of the Project Method

(i) The Project selected for the teaching of Home Science must be significant and have an educative value. They should be according to the capacity and ability of the students.

(ii) The planning should be done by the students.

(iii) Students must assume responsibility and make decisions.

(iv) The whole project should be performed by the students.

(v) Problems for projects must arise in the class-room teaching and class-room discussion.

(vi) The teacher should act as the unseen promoter.

Problem-solving Method

This method generally referred to as Problem Method consists in training the pupils to solve problems. This method is based upon the process of finding out the results by attacking a problem in a number of definite steps. In this method, the student is involved in finding out the answer to a given problem and thus actually it is a discovery method. In the words of Yoakan and Simpson, " a problem occurs in a situation in which a felt-difficulty to act is realised. It is a difficulty that is clearly present and recognised by the thinker. It may be purely mental difficulty or it may be physical and involve the manipulation of data. The distinguishing thing about a problem, however, is that if impresses the individual who meets it as needing a solution."

Procedure : The method proceeds in various steps discussion in the following lines.

Recognising the Problem. First of all, we sense the presence of a problem and then identify the problem.

Defining the Problem. The problem is then defined very precisely and accurately.

Collecting Relevant Data. Then all sorts of relevant data, which can be helpful in solving the problem, are collected and arranged in proper order.

Organising the Data. The data is then organised in such a way that it can lead to the solution of the problem.

Formulating the Tentative Solution. On the basis of the organised data, the student formulates tentative solutions of the problem.

Arriving at the Correct Solution. Out of the tentative solutions, a correct solution is found out by a process of reasoning.

Verifying the Results. In Home Science, we do not accept a conclusion without proper verification. The students are required to verify the conclusion by reversing the process of reasoning.

Merits of Problem-solving Method

(i) It prepares the students in problem-solving. This training in solving-problems is quite useful in solving problems in actual life.

(ii) It stimulates thinking, reasoning and imagination of the students.

(iii) It develops a habit of doing work independently in the students.

(iv) This method of teaching is quite suitable for Home Science as Home Science is full of problems.

(v) It stimulates intellectual curiosity and motivates students to exert further.

(vi) It increases the amount of experience in learning.

(vii) It is based on realistic approach.

(viii) It helps in developing a good relationship between the teacher and the taught.

(ix) It helps the students to learn relationship pattern among things and variables.

(x) It provides the students a training in the methods and skills of discovering new knowledge in Home Science.

Demerits of the Problem-solving Method

(i) It is a long drawn out and time consuming method.

(ii) It is not suitable for all topics in Home Science.

(iii) This method is suitable only for bright and creative students.

(iv) This method is not suitable for students in lower classes.

(v) This method requires special preparation on the part of the teacher. An average teacher may find it difficult to adopt this method.

(vi) The content of Home Science can not be organised according to requirements of this method.

(vii) Suitable text-books for use of this method are not available.

Application : This method trains the pupils in problem-solving. They learn to sense, analyse, reflect, organise and solve the problems. It helps us at every step in our teaching-learning process. The teacher should carefully select the problems which are real and have definite educational values. The teacher should also prepare himself well for the success of the problem-solving method.

Example : Problem. Opening a Cooperative Store : While opening and managing the store, the pupils learn the elements of shopping such as buying, selling, weighing, measuring and preparing bills, preparing budgets, different ways of saving leading to the learning of topics like simple interest, stocks and shares, insurance etc.

Procedure in Problem-solving Method : The teacher should follow either Inductive Procedure or Deductive Procedure while using this method of teaching.

Steps in Inductive Process : It involves the following steps:

(i) Recognising the pattern of the problem,

(ii) Analysing the conditions,

(iii) Organising the information,

(iv) .Farming solutions, and

(v) Eliminating.

Steps in Deductive Process : It involves the following steps:

Understanding the Problem. At the outset, the pupils try to understand the problem and clearly define and formulate it.

Collecting Information. The pupils collect information. This step is not as extensive as in the inductive procedure.

Reviewing. Principles, generalisations, rules etc. are reviewed to find as to which may be applicable to find a suitable solution to the problem.

Drawing Inference. The principle, rule or generalisation is applied to case and inference is drawn that the problem falls under such and such principles.

Verification. The principle is applied to the case. If it solves the problem, well and good otherwise the procedure is repeated to find the correct one.

Merits of the Deductive Method

1. It is short and time saving and so this method is liked by authors and teachers.

2. It is suitable method for lower classes.

3. It glorifies memory because students are required to memorise a large number of laws, formula etc.

4. For revision of topic it is an adequate and advantageous method.

5. It supplements inductive method and thus completes the process of inductive-deductive method.

6. It enhances speed and efficiency in solving problem.

Limitations

(i) It is not a scientific method.

(ii) It encourages rote memory because pure deductive work required some law principle, formula for every type of problem and it demands blind memorisation of large number of such laws/formulas etc.

(iii) Being an unscientific method it does not impart any training in scientific method.

(iv) It causes unnecessary and have burden on the brain which may some times results in brain fag.

(v) In this method memory becomes more important than understanding and intelligence which is educationally not sound.

(vi) It is un-psychological method because the facts and principles are not found by students themselves.

(viii) It is not suitable for development of thinking, reasoning and discovery.

Group Work

Group work, as a method of teaching may be considered as a vice media of collective or class-teaching and the individual work methods. Through this device, the teacher can avoid some of the disadvantages of individual work and include some of the merits of the collective work. It is believed that pupil learn best, when they work together. Therefore, in this method, group work is encouraged in this class-room, library recreation ground etc. When the students are actively engaged in activities and discussions learning becomes interesting and effective.

The types of group work depend upon the classes. The class may be divided into smaller groups according to the ability and interests of the pupils or as the nature or the subject of the solution of common difficulties. The unit becomes smaller and greater individual attention is possible. Over-individualism, as may be the outcome of individual teaching is avoided altogether. For the success of this method planning is being made both by the students and the teachers. Long-term or short-term, small or large, pupil-directed or teacher-directed group should be organised in this method of teaching. The teacher should be fully aware of the proper ways organisation. Ryburn has pointed out the following points to be followed by the teachers while organising group work:

Procedure for Organising and Forming Groups

(i) Groups should be properly graded according to the intelligence and attainments of the students. Defective classification will not make group work effective.

(ii) Every member of the group should take part in the group activities. Its value will be greatly reduced if the leader or the prominent member only monopolise the activities.

(iii) The group should not be needlessly small or large. It should be of convenient size depending on the nature of the work.

(iv) The teacher should properly supervise the work of the group. Over-looking on the part of the teacher may allow the group members shirk work.

(v) There should be no rigidity about membership. According to the progress made or work done, one may be transferred to any other group. Also these group formations should not be only confined to extra-curricular activities. They may pervade all the activities of the class, whether curricular.

From the discussion made above, it is understood that this method only suggests and does not prescribe a single approach to the teaching procedure. The teacher's techniques are always conditioned by the circumstances. She is to be resourceful and adaptive to combine what good she finds to realise her aims. The success of group work depends on how far the teachers is putting heart and soul into her work. Group work is a middle-of-path approach and a wise teacher is to draw out the maximum and the best from its application.

Merits of Group Work

(i) In group work, pupils develop a group feeling and cooperation and healthy competition is encouraged.

(ii) There is scope for the pupils to get training in leadership.

(iii) As the pupils are actively engaged in activities and discussions, learning becomes interesting.

(iv) Learning of a subject becomes effective, when pupils are actively involved in solving problems together.

(v) Disadvantages of too much individualism in the classroom is avoided.

(vi) This method can be successfully applied in reading, spelling, arranging social function, pronunciation and bridging the gap in activities which is occasioned by shortage of materials e.g., lack of suitable books, apparatus and other type of equipment or in carrying out a project.

(vii) Since there is change for exchange of ideas, there is change for the mental development of the pupils.

(viii) Students develop a sense of respect for the ideas and outlook of other individuals.

(ix) Students learn how to adjust to the environment in which they live.

(x) The group work encourages monitorial system within the framework of class, where monitor or the leader of the group can be a little teacher-substitute and can supplement the work of the teacher.

Assignment Method

Literally, the term assignment means the giving out of a task or job by a person in authority. But in the modern art of teaching it has gained a new meaning. In the past more emphasis was given on reproduction through memory, whatever the child either listened from the teacher or read from the books. The feature of a good assignment are as follows:

Features of Good Assignment

(i) It should be related to subject matter under study;

(ii) It should be concise and balanced which can be finished by student easily and quickly;

(iii) Its purpose should be clear and its objective be made known to the students;

(iv) It should be so worded that it fosters thinking and independent learning;

(v) It should be such so as to suit to the age, aptitudes and interest of the student;

(vi) It should be able to combine various methods of teaching.

Teacher's Role : The teacher has to do the following for the success of assignment method of teaching:

(i) He should spilt up the prescribed course in Home Science into successive and progressive assignments;

(ii) He should list down the objective for each assignment which students must achieve;

(iii) He should prepare a progress chart for each student;

(iv) He must prepare and provide a list of reference material required for each assignment;

(v) To cover up the learning gaps he should prepare remedial assignments;

(vi) He should also prepare activity sheets for laboratory work and experiments.

Merits of Assignment Method : This method of teaching has the following advantages:

(i) It provides the students an opportunity for self-study.

(ii) It synthesizes various methods of teaching of science and makes the learning process very effective.

(iii) It provides an opportunity to the student to learn at his own pace and thus the progress of the brighter students is not hindered by weaker students.

(iv) In this system, teacher gets the central role of contingency manager and facilitator of learning. The teacher acts as a guide and interferes least in the student's work.

(v) It places more emphasis on practical work and provides students a training in skill of information processing.

(vi) It provides a feel for the scientific methods to students.

(vii) In this process the learning process can be individualized to a great extent by having differential assignment.

(viii) It provides for corrective feed back and remediation.

(ix) The progress chart with the teacher shows the progress of each student at a glance which gives the teacher an idea of a gifted and weaker students.

(x) In this process, the student learns to work himself because in laboratory he is not provided with any laboratory attendant.

(xi) Habit of extra study is developed because a number of books for extra study are recommended by the teacher. Such a study helps in widening the outlook of the pupil.

(xii) Since the burden of work lies on pupil so he learns to take responsibility.

(xiii) Since the students perform experiments at their own speed so owing to their different speeds they do not perform the same experiment at the same time. Thus, a large quantity of same kind of apparatus is not required.

Disadvantages of Assignment Method : Some of the disadvantages of assignment methods are as follows:

(i) It burdens the teacher with a lot of planning and thus increases his workload to a large extent. It requires the teacher to prepare a well thought out scheme for the year before starting the method.

(ii) No source material is available in the market for assignments preparation of assignments for different students become an uphill task for the teacher.

(iii) The success of method depends on the availability of rich library and laboratory facilities. It makes the method very expensive.

(iv) Before starting with this method teacher must satisfy himself that the apparatus etc. required for practical work are available in the laboratory. He should also satisfy himself about the availability of text books, laboratory manual, notebook etc. and see that each student possesses them.

(v) In this method, teacher gets an opportunity to give individual attention to each pupil.

(vi) Students get an opportunity to work in laboratory.

(vii) Individual progress in learning material are not affected by this method.

Demerits of the Method

(i) Lack of adequate text-books.

(ii) Lack of standard laboratory.

(iii) Lack of facilities of separate reading room.

(iv) Students may copy the work from their friends without doing the work themselves.

(v) It is a lengthy method

Classification of Assignments : Assignments may be classified under two heads (i) Home Assignments (ii) School Assignments.

In home assignments, the teacher gives certain assignments to the students to be worked out at home. She also gives reference from different sources connected with the topic. The students go through different books, journals and other sources and collect necessary information to work out the assignments. After completing the assignments they handover the assignment to the teacher, at school. The teacher verifies them and gives necessary suggestions for further improvement. The students proceed with their work according to the suggestions given by the teacher.

In school assignment, the students perform experiments in the school laboratory. In the school time one third of the period are allotted to Home Science per week for demonstration by the teacher and one-third for individual laboratory work by the students themselves. The teacher makes demonstrations on difficult assignments and simple and easy assignments are performed by the pupils in the laboratory. Thus, they learn things from direct experience in the laboratory. The Home Science teacher gives a sheet of information to the pupils before they start their laboratory work, while answering the questions in the note book, they go through the instructions. They return the note books one day before the beginning of the practical work. Students, who have completed their home assignments are allowed to take part in the practical classes. To evaluate the progress of the students, the teacher maintains a progress card for each student.

Assignment Method

Specimen of Progress Chart

School________ Class________ From ________ To________

No.	*Name of Student*	*Class Test*	*Assignments*	*Term Exam.*	*Remarks*

Conclusion : In spite of the demerits of this method as discussed above, this method is very helpful to the students studying in higher classes. By the help of this method, they acquire sufficient information about the concepts and principles of Home Science. For the success of this method, the teacher plays a vital role. Since preparation of assignment is an art, she must learn this art and apply it in the Home Science laboratory.

Role Playing

In role playing two or more persons attempt to act or do as somebody else has acted or is expected to act at a certain time, in a certain place or situation. It is unrehearsed drama, where the emotion reactions of the people are studied from their spontaneous acting. This method is based on the principle that if someone tries to act out an individual's behaviour, she begins to feel as the individual feels, when she acts that way. Thus she begins to understand her feeling by putting herself in her place. By the help of this method the students can have direct experience of family and social relationships. Therefore, in the teaching of Home Science, this method is of vital importance. It can be effectively used in the Home Science class.

Reading of Home Science text-book, and listening to the Home Science lesson from the mouth of the teacher do not help the students to have direct experience of things. In role playing, when the students get an opportunity to play as if they were really facing a particular social situation, or as if they were persons different from themselves, their understanding goes beyond what is got through reading a book or listening to a teacher. From spontaneeus role-playing of a problem situation, the students not only develop an intellectual understanding of a problem but also experience emotions similar to those felt in the social relations of life. In role playing, the following steps followed:

Steps in Role Playing : The teacher tells the first part of a story about a family. In the middle of the story she stops and asks some one to play out the ending of the story, the way she desires. When the action of the actors starts they do not use any written script or portions to be memorised. Each actor is told about role of the character she is to play in the story. She has just to act and talk the way she thinks that character would act and say in her real life situation. Thus throughout this socio-drama students freely express their opinions. As a result of which learning becomes effective, interesting and real.

Advantages of Role Playing

(i) In this method, there is chance for the development of the power of self-creativeness and activity of the children.

(ii) It is play way in the teaching of Home Science. Pupils acquire knowledge.

(iii) Through this method, we can develop the speaking ability of the students.

(iv) Pupils are able to understand the problems faced by the people in the family and in the society.

(v) They learn how to tackle problems in a realistic and interesting way.

(vi) Pupils learn to identify themselves with the adults living in the family.

(vii) Pupils learn to study and understand their own behaviour and behaviour of others.

Disadvantages of Role Playing

Though role playing is an effective method of teaching Home Science, there are certain difficulties in implementing it. Some of the disadvantages of this method are given below:

(i) This method requires some technical knowledge, which most of our teacher lack. It can be applied by those gifted teacher who have sufficient background and training.

(ii) It is a time-consuming device. It may not be possible to devote so much time to complete a prescribed course.

(iii) All the topics of Home Science cannot be taught by the help of this method.

Even if the method is not free from defects, it is unanimously agreed that it is quite a successful and effective method of teaching Home Science. In order to implement this method effectively and successfully the teacher should be careful about the following facts:

(i) The actors should not be felt-conscious before the group while playing their respective roles.

(ii) They should try to project themselves fully as and when a situation is not real to them.

(iii) They should be spontaneous.

(iv) The group should try to get into the spirit of role-playing in order to discuss the problem after the drama is over.

(v) Role playing should not be either over-used or frequently used or inappropriately used.

(vi) It should not be used for the development of the physical skills of the pupils. It should be used only to develop an understanding of the feeling of others.

Teaching is an art and the teacher is an artist. An individual becomes a real teacher even if he possesses the required degree from a recognised university. Therefore, the educationists all over the world have devised and are devising from time to time according to their philosophic background and universally accepted psychological and educational principles, certain methods of teaching procedures. Education is a dynamic science and more and more contributions to it are making it richer and richer day by day. New method of teaching with definite procedures are coming into vogue with the changed and modernised concepts. No one method can be recommended for use in teaching any particular lesson of Home Science. The success of these methods depend upon the end product of teaching, the result of instruction, in times of pupil growth and development. An effective method of teaching Home Science is one which is flexible and workable. It must not be stereotyped. It must suit to different situations. Hence different situations demand different methods. A good method of teaching is one, which makes teaching interesting, functional continuous and easily acquired. An effective teacher can hope to direct her pupils towards the aims and objectives of Home Science successfully, if and when she follows the correct method. It must be remembered that there is no one best method of teaching Home Science. A successful teacher of Home Science is one who is familiar with all methods of teaching

Home Science, but who selects the one which suits her best at a particular time and place, for directing the learning process towards the achievement of the aims and objectives.

QUESTIONS

1. Which is the most effective method of teaching Home Science? Give a comparative account of other methods.

2. Write short note on Project and Assignment method.

3. Explain the various methods of teaching and write about the best suitable method to teach.

4. How will you organise an effective demonstration to teach the subject of cookery.

5. Explain the effectiveness of Project Method in teaching Home Science at Secondary level.

6. What do you understand by demonstration method? What points would you keep into mind to make your demonstration a success?

7. How can a successful discussion can be conducted on a particular topic in the class?

8. How can effective learning be imparted in the laboratories? Discuss in detail.

9. How can an effective demonstration be carried out?

10. What do you know about the discussion? How far this method of teaching is successful one.

8

Teaching Principles

Skinner has said that teaching is an art as well as science. Since science is a systematic and scientific process, teaching is also based on certain principles. For effective teaching, it is must for the teachers to be aware of these principles. These principles are necessary for controlling and altering the behaviour of the pupils. These principles can be classified into two categories:

1. General principles of teaching

2. Psychological principles of teaching

General Principles

Principle of Definite Objective: Every field of study provides us with knowledge. To provide knowledge it is must for the teacher to set some objective or goal. These objectives are general and specific. They help the teacher to choose the right path and not to deviate from that path. General aim of Home Science teacher is to help students become good housewives and through specific objectives they prepare them in various fields of the study as Foods and Nutrition, Human Development, Clothing and Textiles, Home Management. Within these each specific field also in-depth study is required e.g. Human Development. This branch studies all aspects of the human being from conception till death in detail. The teacher must be clear about the aim of knowledge to be imparted to the students since his teaching methods are to be based on these objectives.

Principle of Individual Differences: Every student is different in intelligence, nature, aptitudes, abilities, interest, background and needs. Thus, the requirement of each child differs. It becomes responsibility of the teacher to see that every type of student is benefitted from his teaching methods. In general knowledge, is imparted taking average student into consideration. Extra material is provided to the bright students and for weaker students extra classes are conducted.

Principle of Selection: Today knowledge is expanding at vast speed. Content of knowledge to be imparted has to be selected according to set objectives and mental abilities of the students. Man has collected huge and complex knowledge in every subject. If teacher tends to impart all knowledge to the students he would rather confuse them and they would not be able to understand the essence of the subject matter. Based on the objectives and mental level of the pupils some things are essential and some are non-essential. Non-essential knowledge does not benefit students. Teacher should clearly select what and how much is to be taught. For this, clear, definite and set objectives are required. Also the teacher must understand the psychology of the students. This will benefit both the teachers and the pupils. Teachers can prepare lesson carefully and student would acquire it easily and conveniently.

Principle of Interest: For useful and effective teaching, it is necessary that student is interested in the subject matter. When the student takes interest in the subject matter learning becomes easy for him. For creating interest in a particular subject, the teacher should adopt the various methods :

(i) The aims, objectives and content of the subject matter should be clear to the teacher and the taught to avoid confusions.

(ii) Contents of the subject matter should be based on the objectives of the concerned field and mental abilities of the students..

(iii) Subject should be taught by learning by doing method.

(iv) Subject should be linked with daily activities and active life of the pupils.

The Principle of Activity or Learning by Doing: Just lecturing the students becomes useless many times. If the students learn anything by doing themselves they are bound to learn easily and memorise it for a longer period. In the beginning, Froebel emphasised the importance of learning by doing. This method was applied at 'Kindergarten level'. Learning becomes easier, quicker and effective if child is physically and mentally active in the class room. e.g., merely memorising the color schemes and furniture arrangement in the room is not sufficient. The students will forget the proper placement of furniture articles in the room. But when the room plan is drawn on the paper or actual arrangements are done in the room the real image will remain in the mind for a longer period. While conducting lessons in Foods it is always better when students plan and cook food articles themselves. In Clothing and Textiles when cutting and stitching is done with own hands, learning becomes effective and permanent.

In the middle and high classes, the principle may be applied in a large variety of forms, e.g., the use of assignment and the Dalton plan. Here the pupils themselves find out the answers to questions by studying a number of books, looking up references and discussing topics with experts, teachers and class-mates. In Heuristic method, the pupils do not learn facts passively but have to be mentally alive and alert in the process of finding out the truth.

For helping the students in learning by doing cottage is planned for Home Science students. Here the students play the role of home maker in every aspect. She has to play the role of cook, host, dishwasher, accounts keeper, gardener, consumer etc. Conducting of various roles gives the child opportunity of learning desirable attitude by doing.

The Principle of Connecting with Life: Subject should be linked with life as far as possible. Some topics can be easily linked up with life and environment of the student e.g., topic of Hygiene and Physiology in Home Science; small saving schemes where a homemaker can invest her money, planning and stitching of various types of dresses; selecting and buying different kinds of furniture and furnishings; planning, selecting, cooking and storing food items from various food groups etc. Unreal problems make subjects uninteresting e.g., teaching psychological problems of children. If the students are asked to observe same problems in children, it will enhance their observation and will add to practical knowledge. They would learn to find the causes and solutions to the physical, psychological, emotional and mental problems existing among the different sections of the society. The pupils lose interest and get a wrong idea of subjects and topics if they are far removed from life. The current topic of Environmental Education added in syllabus has contributed much in making students become aware of and take interest in their surroundings.

Principle of Motivation: Motivation creates student's interest in a particular field. In the absence of proper motivation, the pupil takes no interest in memorizing the content. This leads to failure of teaching. The teacher can exploit the innate tendencies of students through motivation. For this short-term and end-term examinations are conducted and the toppers are rewarded. Many times discussions, debates and different kinds of competitions are organized in the educational institutions. When a student fares better he feels motivated to do better. Motivation can be given in the form of material products e.g., rewards etc. It can also take the form of praise, approval, promotion, special favours etc. Motivation can be 'inner' also. When a student feels that learning a particular thing will benefit his life or a particular kind of learning is linked to his daily life, he feels 'self motivated'. Then he develops interest in that field and tries to learn it in a better sense.

Principle of Planning: In the teaching process, proper planning is required. For this teacher should plan the teaching sequence and after proper planning the lesson-plan should be prepared. Teaching should proceed from simple to complex stage. It should also be taken into consideration at which stage the co-operation and help of pupils can be taken e.g., some topics which require imagination or data collection or general type can be given to the students in assignment form. For some topics students can be asked to prepare models. Planning of teaching sequence makes teaching much simpler for the teachers since it makes aware of many problems which can be aroused at the time of teaching. Many times a problem arises at the time of teaching which had never been imagined. In such a situation teacher can solve that problem according to his ability.

Principle of Division: According to this principle whole of teaching matter should be divided into some units for presenting it in certain order. The total subject matter should be divided in units in such a way that each unit is complete in itself and covers a particular topic wholly. These units proceed from simpler to complex form. This makes learning easy for pupils and they become curious about the subject-matter in preceeding units.

Principle of Revision: The taught subject matter if not revised tends to the forgotten. Without utilizing or revising the acquired knowledge it starts decreasing from the memory. Revision can be done in units or in whole depending upon the length and complexity of subject-matter. More complex and difficult subject matter needs immediate and repeated repetitions. The subject matter which is general and related to day-to-day environment needs less of repetitions. More technical knowledge tends to be forgotten thus requires thorough repetitions.

Principle of Creation and Recreation: Knowledge which is creative and recreational is always interesting for the pupils. This type of teaching enhances creative abilities of the students. In this type of learning, students take interest without fear of teacher and the school. They will try for new innovations and they will have an opportunity of expressing creative activities. Modern teaching methods are based on 'play-way' or re-creative methods like teaching of alphabets, numerals and other things through poems, rhymes, music etc. Helping students express their inner creative potentialities through paintings, model making, modelling, speeches, writing, dramatisation etc. make teaching much effective.

Principle of Democratic Dealing: According to this principle attitude of teacher towards students should be democratic not dictatorial. Democratic attitude allows for free expression of abilities and potentialities while in dictatorship personality gets repressed. Self-expression is enhanced in democratic setup thus adding to balanced personality traits. Teacher should adopt cordial relations with the pupils while planning and teaching lessons. Such type of assignments should be given that help in independent thinking and allow free expression of ideas. In exams such type of questions should be asked which require for subjective answering. Answers should not be limited to a particular alternative although this is not applicable in technical subjects. Subjects like Home Science allows for the maximum creative expression. Teachers should ask maximum questions and as many alternatives to the problem should be encouraged as possible. This creates the habit of thinking independently in the pupils. It also creates the merits like self-confidence, self-esteem, self-respect in their personality.

Principles of Correlating with other Subjects: The main principle of learning is to prepare the child for the future and help him adjust in his life. Most of the subjects are related to each other e.g., Home Science being allied subject is related to various other fields like Physiology, Economics, Psychology, Microbiology, Biochemistry, Sociology, Physics, Chemistry, Genetics, Statistics etc. All these subjects are interrelated. Study of all these fields should be correlated properly to impart knowledge properly. It utilises efforts, energy and time of the teacher and the learner.

Principle of Lffective Strategies and Instructional Material: For efficient teaching effective modes of teaching and instructional materials are required. The selection of strategies and instructional materials depend upon the specific subject, the unit of subject to be taught and mental abilities of the students. Every method of teaching is not effective in all circumstances. For Maths instructional material can be books; for Science this material can be books, models, computers; for Home Science this could be books, lectures, practicals demonstrations, field studies etc.

Principle of Cooperation: Teaching and learning is a cooperative and joint effort. Here cooperation is required between teachers, students, parents, authorities of the institution and the persons involved in the formulation of policies regarding education. Even if one agency is not helpful, it would create hindrance in the working of the institution.

Principle of Model Presentation: Teacher should be conscious that the teaching matter presented in the class is model. The personality of the teacher, his behaviour, work should be a model to the students. Teacher is ideal to the students. They imitate his way of speaking, language, way of working, stress-up etc. Teacher should be honest, sincere, sympathatic, truthful and punctual in his behaviour. Only then he can influence his students in proper way.

Psychological Principles

Principle of Activity or Learning by Doing: According to Rousseau, child is a 'hero' in the drama of education and as such he must be allowed to play the dominant role. Thus the progressive educational theories should be based upon the student activity.

Nature has provided the children with great vitality. They are required to be provided with a positive purpose so that energy and vitality can be channelized in the proper direction. Thus, it becomes necessary that children should be provided with the activities that are interesting to them, they should develop the observational nature and explore the environment so that they learn themselves. It adds to the feeling of satisfaction and fulfilment.

To develop the personality of the children it is must that he should explore all his potentialities and become active in all the ways.

Principle of Playway: This principle is very much close to the principle of activity. Froebel has said that play is the main activity of children. It provides happiness, freedom, satisfaction and peace. It holds the source of all that is good. But without rational conscious guidance childhood activity degenerates into aimless play instead of preparing for those tasks of life for which it is designed.

Play is natural activity for the child. To play child need not learn the rules and regulations. This activity comes from within. It is a voluntary activity and it is manifestation of creative urge.

This spirit of play way should prevail in the classroom so that the learning becomes enjoyable activity for the children not just the drudgery.

Principle of Motivation: Motivation plays the major role in teaching process. Motivation makes the child active. It develops the coordination between child and the environment. Motivation is a process through which the inner energy or necessities of the learner are directed towards the purposeful activities of the environment. Efforts, interests, reactions all are results of motivation. Every effort of a human being which wants to attain a goal is motivated. Learning process is coordination of motives and goals.

Motivation is developed through the motivators. Motivators are those physical and mental conditions of any human being which attract him to perform a particular work.

Principle of Self-education: Best type of education is one in which children learn by their own efforts. Teachers should initiate the imagination in children. Children should explore the material and environment themselves and express themselves freely. Teacher's role should be just to guide and provide necessary help wherever required but not to interfere. He should stand aside and watch. He must talk less, explain less and direct less. Adamson states: The whole business is between the individual and his world's and the teacher is outside it, external to it. He may facilitate it, turning his attention to one or other member of the wedded pair. He may approach the individual and his avenues of approach will be one or other of the instincts or emotional dispositions which are the prime movers of the mental life. He may try fear, pugnacity, curosity, or sympathy or a combination of them, to quickness the current which seem to him sluggish or he may approach the fact or truth, whichever of the these words it belongs to, and see whether anything can be done by lightning it up, or lining in main features and blothing out detail to facilitate adjustment. But whatever he tries, subject or object or both together, he remains outside the process, a spectator, a manipulator, perhaps a disturber; he is never in it and of it. Within that mysterious synthetic activity through which the individual is at once appropriating and contributing to his environment, forming and being formed by it.... the teacher has neither place nor part." According to this statement in teaching, it is not essential that child should adjust to the teacher but he should become capable of adjusting to the environment and to change the environment to adjust himself. Teaching should make the child independent.

As stated by Dr. A.G. Hughes and Dr. E.H. Hughes, "Teachers are not superfluous and teaching is not the baneful evil. It is true that children are curious, assertive and creative by nature but also they are submissive, imitative and ready to appeal for help. Thus teaching is required for children. But we must know when to teach children and when to stand aside, when to explain and when to leave children to make discoveries, when to demonstrate and when to leave children free to experiment, when to require children to listen and when to provide for free expression." The teacher should inspire the children to develop enthusiasm for the learning. He should develop natural desires and guide these desires into worth-while channels.

Principle of Individual Differences: Since every individual differs in his physical, mental, psychological potentialities, thus teaching must be such so as to cover the individual differences of children.

Principle of Goal Setting: In teaching, definite goals should be set so that child is clear what is expected of him. For smaller children short term goals could be there but as the child grows long term goals can be set. Child should be clear about these goals so that he is not ambiguous in his expectations.

Principle of Repetition and Exercise: If the learning material is carefully read and repeated many times, it is remembered. Repetition does not means cramming rather coordination should be established between the learning material and after understanding the material it should be remembered. Repetition after useful understanding is always useful. After learning many times memory traces are deepened and material is remembered for a longer period.

Principle of Change, Rest and Recreation: One kind of learning material becomes monotonous after some time. Teacher should plan his teaching material in such a way that some change is provided in-between. The students should be given enough rest. Some recreation in-between of teaching like reciting some poem, song, telling some joke or life experience provides the atmosphere of freshness.

Principle of Feed Back and Reinforcement: Immediate knowledge of the result helps the child in judging where does he stand and what is his progress in life. By coming to know of his position he may attempts to enhance it. Reinforcements like certificates, praise, providing prestigious position in the class or group like appointing monitor, president of a club or other material reward helps in making the task of learning enjoyable.

Principle of Sympathy and co-operation: A good teacher not only provides the education but acts as a guide. He provides sympathetic, co-operative and cordial atmosphere and helps him to progress in life. He mixes with the students and develops their faith. Students can establish full confidence in their teachers and do not hesitate in removing their difficulties and problems. Teaching method is not effective till a teacher wins the confidence and faith of the students. Cordial atmosphere creates the educative and active atmosphere in the class.

Principle of Providing Training to Senses: Nature has provided the human beings with five senses-sight, smell, taste, touch and hearing. Education should utilize these senses to attain good results in education. Coordination of these senses helps in making the education easier. Observation, inspection, exploration, discrimination, generalisation, application, perception identification, experimentation etc. all abilities require the proper development and training of senses. For the best results, the teacher should develop co-ordination and utilize the senses of children.

Principle of Utilizing Group Dynamics: Group behaviour influences the individual behaviour very much. Internal activities, outside activities and attitude of the group create a particular kind of teaching atmosphere for the child. These behaviours have positive or negative influences on the child. It creates a particular kind of atmosphere for the child. A good teacher should take the whole atmosphere into consideration and a suitable climate for group dynamics should be created in the classroom environment.

Principle of Effect: Any learning is strengthened if followed by pleasure and weakened if followed by displeasure.

Principle of Exercise: The more the learned material is repeated the more it is strengthened and retained for a longer period. If any stimulus is not repeated, the bond is weakened between situation and response.

Principle of Creativity: Teacher should provide the maximum opportunity to the students to explore the environment and find out the cause-effect relationship. Inner potentialities of the child should be explored to the maximum and he should be allowed to express himself.

Principle of Correlation: Teaching should be correlated with the work and task. It should not be only theoretical rather it should be linked with the physical and social environment.

Principle of Remedial Teaching: Education should change the student and lead him to the progress. It should identify and remove the individual and group shortcomings and difficulties of the children. If the student need individual guidance and special attention, it becomes the duty of the teachers to provide for the necessary help and coaching.

QUESTIONS

1. Discuss the various methods of approach of teaching.
2. What are the different principles of a good teaching method?
3. Which principle should be followed to make the teaching learning process more effective?

9

Teaching Aids

It is now a well recognised fact that to keep teaching interesting and make it effective we have to make use of certain material aids. The use of these material aids makes teaching effective, simple and interesting.

In the past, most teaching depended almost entirely upon verbal communication to the student, or written communication to the student from printed materials. Although these communication channels continue to play important roles in the learning process, today's students are learning facts, skills and attitudes from pictures, television, recorded words, programmed lessons and other media. Though the use of sensory aids in teaching is of recent origin, we have been using text-books, blackboard etc. since long . All these are now considered as sensory aids. For many years resourceful teachers have been using models, instruments, drawing and other desires for stimulating interest and to facilitate the learning process. For teaching of Home Science we require various teaching aids and in the pages to follow an attempt will be made to discuss various teaching aids that are used in teaching of Home Science.

Place in Home Science

Teaching involves communication of ideas or knowledge. The object of modern schooling is to provide for the necessary and desirable experiences for the children within a limited time and in specified fields. It depends upon the successful planning of these experiences to be provided for and bringing them within the realisation by the children. Teaching aids help to make abstract ideal less abstract or complete ideas less complex. Teacher takes the help of various teaching aids. Teaching aids influence the minds of the learners through their senses the use of audio-visual aids makes learning experiences concrete and meaningful, makes understanding quicker and greater. There is an increase in interesting and improvement in attitudes. The aids and materials which help our senses of hearing and seeing to learn more effectively and efficiently are called audio-visual aids.

Audio-visual aids have entered into the teaching process to a large extent and some of these are of such paramount importance in ensuring proper grasp of the subject and developing power of imagination that some of them at least deserve special treatment. The teacher of Home Science is expected to exploit audio-visual aids since they offer immense scope to economy and effectiveness of teaching efforts. About these aids Comenius says, "The foundation of all teaching consists in representing clearly of the senses, sensible objects, so that they can be appreciated easily." The audiovisual aids can maintain an accelerated tempo in class-room instructions of Home Science in various ways. Some of the these are as follows:

(i) They provided an opportunity to the teacher for freshness of his presentation and so greater incentive to learning the subject.

(ii) They help in clear understanding of the subject and in clarifying the abstract ideas.

(iii) They appeal the senses of the pupils and so they satisfy their innate tendencies and interests.

(iv) They bring the pupils indirect contact with objects and things.

(v) They bring near what is distant.

(vi) By bringing the world into the class-room they help the child in understanding different cultural background.

(vii) They stimulate pupil participation. They are based on the maxim 'learning by doing'.

(vii) They make teaching-learning process interesting.

(ix) They help in saving time and energy because it takes a long time to clarify an abstract idea verbally but the point can be made clear at once by using some appropriate teaching aid.

(x) The need of individual students are met. Some pupil learn by listening but a majority of them by doing.

(xi) They help in creating a lasting impression on the mind of the learner. Things are well retained in the mind since the sensory impressions are more permanent.

Various Types

Audio-visual aids can be classified as under:

Visual Aids : It refers to those aids that catch the eyes, e.g., charts, maps, pictures, black-board, flannel-board, epidiascope, slides, films strips etc.

Audio Aids : It refers to those aids that catch the ears, e.g., tape-recorder, gramophone records etc.

Audio-visual Aids : These are the aids that catch the eyes and ears, e.g., Television, films etc.

Dr. Edgar Dale has classified and arranged audio-visual aids in a proctorial form called "Cone of experience".

Cone of Experience : We all agree that the senses arc the primary source of contact between the individual and external world and any intellectual activity depends on experiences coming through senses. Even mental activities such as concentration, reflection, conception, imagination, association, recollection etc. have their basis in sensory experiences. Mind like stomach, works on what it is fed. This feeding comes through senses. The raw material for mental activity is provided by.

Direct Experiences: Such experiences are gained by the pupils through excursions and trips etc.

Representative Experiences: This type of experiences are less concrete but are quite useful. This type of experiences are provided by models, specimens, film strips, radio etc.

Verbal and Symbolic Experiences: Such experiences are those which the pupils gain through word-oral or written. This type of experiences are very abstract and occur at conceptual level e.g.

verbal illustrations. This type of experience can not be properly followed at the initial stages of child-learning so at initial stage more emphasis be laid on direct and representative experiences.

In the picture below are shown various experiences:

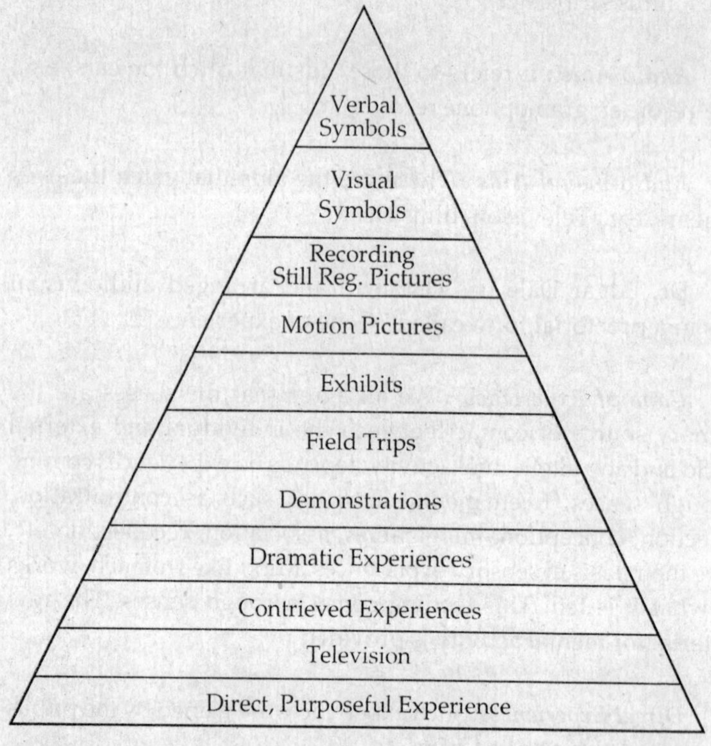

Edge Dale's Cone of Experience.

The above cone represents the material used for audio-visual instructions.

The theory of audio-visual instruction needs that education must make learning permanent and experiences usable. The advocacy for the use of new material for improving instructions is based on the fact that the verbalistic learning is out of date and the complexity of the time has made our school curriculum very much heavy as the present day knowledge has developed tremendously. We need new ways to adjust ourselves to the changed circumstances and the trends towards realistic learning.

The Source

There are many sources of audio-visual material. Among them the Home Science room itself is a good source of actual material to be used as teaching aids. An ideal Home Science room consists of the best learning materials available for units on equipments, pictures, utensils, decorations, etc.

It is very necessary to keep some audio-visual aids for the purpose of teaching, different areas of home-making. Quite a large number of effective and useful teaching aids can be prepared by the teachers and their students. It provides an effective learning experience to the students. Besides these some materials may be collected from shops, homes and the community. The toys used by the children, picture, utensils, textiles, furniture etc. are some of the useful teaching aids for the teaching of Home Science.

Audio-visual aids may also be collected from the State and Central Government Department of Education. Information and Broadcasting, Education organisations, Red-cross, etc. Without much difficulty a teacher may collect teaching aids such as pamphlets, charts, maps, graphs, exhibits etc. But educational films, film strips may be collected from the Ministry of Education, Health, and Community development. If possible some aids may be purchased by the school from different agencies at concessional rates. An ideal teacher of Home Science should try best to collect the audio-visual materials from all available sources.

Various Kinds

The Black Board/Chalk Board : It is one of the most common visual aids in use. Black board forms an integral part of class-room. Black board is a slightly abrasive writing surface made of wood, ply, hard board, bluish paint on it. This board is used by the teacher to draw sketches, maps, diagrams etc. It is also used by the teacher to put down the substance of the chapter or the topic taught. Through black board, it is possible to develop the chapter or the topic taught.

A chalk board is generally installed facing the class which is either built into the wall or fixed and framed on the wall and provided with a ledge to keep the chalk sticks and duster. Portable chalk boards are also available these days. Such chalk boards can be placed on a stand with adjustable height. Generally white chalk sticks are used for writing on the black board or chalk board but some time coloured chalk sticks are also used. The coloured chalk sticks are used for better illustration.

Characteristics of a Good Chalk Board : Some of the characteristics of a good chalk board are as follows :

(i) Its surface should be rough enough so that it is capable of holding the writing on the board.

(ii) Its surface should be dull so that it can eliminate glare.

(iii) Its surface should be such that the writing on the board can be easily removed by making use of a cloth or a foam duster.

(iv) Its height should be so adjusted that it is within the easy reach of the teacher and is easily visible to the students.

Effective Use of Chalk-Board : We find that chalk board is the most common teaching aid used by the teacher for writing important points, drawing illustrations, solving problems etc. The teacher should keep the following points in mind to use the chalk board effectively.

(i) Write in a clear and legible handwriting the important points on the chalk board but avoid over crowding of information on the chalk board.

(ii) The size of the words written on black board should be such that they can be seen even by the back-benchers. The letters should not be less than one inch in height. The recommended height of letters on a chalk board is between 6 cm to 8 cm. For this, the teacher should frequently inspects his own chalk board writing from the view point of the back-bench on a corner seat.

(iii) There should be proper arrangement of light in the class-room so that the chalk board remains glare free.

(iv) To emphasise some points or parts of a sketch or a diagram coloured chalks be used.

(v) Rub off the information already discussed in the class and noted down by the students.

(vi) Draw a difficult illustration beforehand to save the class time.

(vii) Stand on one side of the chalk board while explaining some points to the students.

(viii) Make use of a pointer for drawing attention to the written material on the chalk board.

(ix) Students may be allowed to express their ideas on chalk board, or to make alterations or corrections. Some times teacher may intentionally draw some incorrect diagram and ask the students to make necessary correction, alteration etc.

(x) For maintenance of proper discipline in the class, the teacher should always keep eye on his class while writing on the black board.

(xi) For proper writing on chalkboard the chalk stick be broken into two pieces and the broken end of the piece be used to start writing.

(xii) While writing on a chalkboard keep your fingers and wrist stiff and move your arm freely.

Advantages of Challk-board : Some of the advantages of chalk board over other visual aids are as follows:

(i) It is very convenient teaching aid for group teaching.

(ii) It is quite economic and can be used again and again.

(iii) Its use is accompanied by the appropriate actions on the part of the teacher. The illustrations drawn on the blackboard captures students, attention.

(iv) It is one of the most valuable supplementary teaching aid.

(v) It can be used as a good visual aid for drill and revision.

(vi) These boards can be used for drawing enlarged illustrations from the text books.

(vii) It is convenient aid for giving lesson notes to the students.

Limitations of the Chalk-board : Some of the important limitations of a chalk board are as under:

(i) The use of chalk-board makes students very much dependent on the teacher.

(ii) It makes the lesson teacher paced.

(iii) It makes the lesson dull and of routine nature.

(iv) It gives no attention to the individual needs of the students.

(v) Due to constant use chalk boards become smooth and start glaring.

(vi) While using chalk-sticks to write on chalk board the teacher spreads a lot of chalk powder which is inhaled by teacher and students and it may affect their health.

Bulletin Boards

It is a display board on which learning material on some geographical topic is displayed. It is generally of the size of a black-board but some times even bigger depending on the wall space available. It is generally in the form of a frame soft-board or straw-board or cork-board or rubber sheets. Such bulletin boards can be specified for individual branches of geography or even for some specified topics, e.g., puzzles, news, cartoons etc. Such aboard can also be used for displaying the best work of students. However, for all purpose bulletin board, the following type of display material is recommended:.

(i) Interesting news;

(ii) Book Jackets of recently published Home science books;

(iii) Brochures;

(iv) Cartoons;

(v) Poems;

(vi) Sketches;

(vii) Pictures;

(viii) Photographs;

(ix) Thoughts;

(x) Announcements etc.

An effort be made to change the material on bulletin board as frequently as is practicable. Whenever the teacher starts a new topic he may ask the students to display the concerned material on the bulletin board and the teacher should specifically mention to the students the display material on the bulletin board while teaching a topic to the class. Students be asked to take the charge of bulletin board by rotation.

How to Use a Bulletin Board ? To make use of bulletin board as a useful teaching aid the bulletin board be used for creating interest amongst students on specific topics. For effective use of bulletin board as a teaching aid following points be kept in mind:

(i) Effort be made jointly by the teacher and the students to procure material from various sources on given subject or topic.

(ii) Before displaying the material on the board, sort out the material relevant to a specific subject or topic.

(iii) Make best use of your aesthetic sense to display the material on the bulletin board.

(iv) Do fix a title for the specific subject/ topic of display material on the top centre of the bulletin board.

(v) It is desirable if a brief description about the specific subject or topic is fixed below the title.

(vi) The height of bulletin board from ground level be about 1 m.

(vii) The bulletin board be fixed in an area where enough lighting can be provided.

(viii) The material displayed should be large enough and should be provided with suitable headings.

(xi) Over crowding of material on bulletin board be avoided.

Advantages of Bulletin Boards : Some of the advantages of bulletin board as teaching aid are as a follows:

(i) It is a good supplement to class-room teaching.

(ii) It helps in arousing the interest of students in a specific subject/ topic.

(iii) It can be effectively used as a follow-up of chalk-board.

(iv) Such boards add colour and liveliness and thus also have decorative value in addition to their educational value.

(v) Such boards can be conveniently used for introducing a topic and for its review as well.

Limitations of Bulletin Board : Some limitations in the use of bulletin boards as teaching aids are as follows:

(i) They cannot be used for all inclusive teaching.

(ii) They can be used only as supplementary aids to some other teaching aid.

(iii) At times it becomes very difficult to make proper selection of the display material for certain topic.

Flannel Board

It is also some times referred to as flannel graph or felt board. It is made of wood, card-board or straw-board covered with coloured flannel or woollen cloth. It is one of the latest devices used for geography teaching. Display materials like cut-outs, pictures, drawing and light objects backed with rough surfaces like sand paper strips flannel strips etc. will stick to flannel board temporarily.

For display purposes a flannel board 1.5 x 1.5 m is generally used. It can be fixed next to the black-board or can be placed on a stand about one metre above the ground.

How to Use a Flannel Board ? Following points be kept in mind for effective use of flannel board as a teaching aid:

(i) The teacher should collect a large number of pictures or wall cut diagrams etc. and back them with sandpaper pieces. He may then make use of these by displaying these on the board one by one, after proper selection.

(ii) Display the material on the flannel board in a sequence to develop the lesson.

(iii) Make proper use of flannel board for creating proper scenes and designs relevant to the lesson.

(iv) Change the display material on the board as frequently as required.

(v) Flannel board can be used quite effectively for showing relationship between different parts or steps of a process.

Advantages of Flannel-Board : Some of the advantages of using flannel-board as a teaching aid are as follows:

(i) It is quite economical and easy to handle and operate.

(ii) The picture or cuttings can be easily fixed and removed when required, without spoiling the material. Thus, same material can be used·for display many a times.

(iii) Any display material on the board holds the interest of students and arrests their attention.

(iv) Such boards enable a teacher to talk along with changing illustrations to develop a lesson.

Magnetic Chalk Board : It is a framed iron sheet having porcelain coating in black or green colour. Such a board can be used either to write with chalk sticks, glass marking pencils and crayons or to display pictures, cut-outs and light objects with disc magnetic holders.

Thus, such a board functions both as a chalk board and as a flannel board. We can display visual learning material on such a board while writing key points on it. Such a board provides the flexibility of movement of visual material. It is possible to display even a three dimensional object on such a board using magnetic holders.

Since the magnetic chalk-board functions both as a chalk board and as a flannel board so various points discussed for the effective use of these boards be kept in mind while using magnetic chalk board as an effective teaching aid.

Advantages of Magnetic Chalk Board : Some of the advantages of magnetic chalk board are as follows:

(i) It is a versatile teaching aid that combines the advantages of both a chalk board and a flannel board.

(ii) It is possible to move visual material by sliding it along the surface of the board such a movement is not possible on a flannel board.

(iii) It is very light and can be easily taken from one place to another.

(iv) Such a board can be easily got prepared in the school from an iron sheet and painting with some good paint.

Charts : Charts also are an important teaching aids. Sometimes charts are needed by the teacher to supplement his actual teaching. There are certain charts which represent a statistical diagram for a series of diagram which may be difficult to understand. Charts require less efforts for presenting the slides.

Following points be kept in view while using charts as teaching aids:

(i) An effort be made to use charts prepared by students under the guidance of the teacher, however some charts may be purchased.

(ii) Only such charts be purchased which have both lines and in which such colours are used as could be seen and distinguished even by the back-benchers.

(iii) Charts should give the essential details.

(iv) Charts should be properly and clearly labelled in block letters.

Sources for Procurement of Charts

(i) Charts can be prepared by students and teacher.

(ii) Charts can be purchased.

(iii) Charts can be procured on a very nominal cost from the following sources:

(a) Ministry of Education, Govt. of India, Delhi.

(b) NCERT, New Delhi.

(c) Director, Extension Service of College of Education in the State.

(d) SCERT of the state.

(e) District Public Relation Officer.

Advantages of Charts

(i) They can be made quickly.

(ii) They have a better appeal.

(iii) Only the essential can be shown in the chart and unnecessary details can be avoided.

(iv) Charts are available from Various sources.

Pictures

To understand the physical and social activities of man in the background of his physical and natural environments pictures are quite useful. The underlying idea of use of pictures was realised by Commensus in his book Orbis Pictures. In geography the eruption of a volcano can be easily explained with the help of a picture. Making use of a picture we can present abstract things in concrete form. Picture help the student in strengthening his knowledge. Pictures give a clearer picture of social and cultural background of the people of a particular country.

Pictures are cheap, easy to produce and store. The teacher can seek the cooperation of students in collection of pictures. Pictures show objects in their natural surroundings. They are - more useful in individual study than a class study.

Though pictures are quite useful teaching aids but it is not possible to present every thing in the form of a picture.

Important Sources of Pictures

(i) Magazines : Educational magazines.

(ii) Official Publications: Publications of Govt. Voices.

(iii) Newspapers and Periodicals.

(iv) Advertising brouchers insured by railways, shipping companies, airlines etc.

v) Discarded books and magazines.

(vi) Postage stamps.

Characteristics of Pictures used in Home Science : The pictures used in geography should have the following characteristics:

1. They should be accurately and neatly drawn.

2. They should be attractive and natural.

3. They should be designed in such a way that there may be places for questions to be put by the teacher to the students.

4. They should carry correct head lines and be upto date.

5. An effort be made to draw a picture in natural background.

Principles for use of Pictures : The following principles be kept in mind for successful use of pictures for teaching of geography:

1. Keep an index and a file of pictures.

2. Large pictures be got mounted on wooden frame of plywood and small pictures be got mounted on butter muslin. It helps to minimise the wear and tear of pictures.

3. Use some projecting machine when you want to display a small size picture.

4. The teacher should explain to the students the things to be studied in a picture.

5. Students be allowed free access to the pictures.

6. After showing a picture the teacher should ask questions which would help to strengthen the knowledge of students and would also sharpen their memory and enrich their imagination.

7. Pictures should be bold, direct and sufficiently large.

8. Pictures should not be over loaded with information rather they should stick to the maximum 'one picture, one idea'.

Cartoons

It is possible to use cartoons as teaching aids. In some cases, they prove quite effective in producing the desired results. In cartoons we depict a story metaphorically and it carries more weight in comparison to a direct statement. The symbolism of cartoons tell its message. Cartoons are very much liked by young children. Cartoon is always for or against some thing and it may be one sided in many a case and if so it may exaggerate or belittle some aspects of the topic. As a teaching aid, it has both its strength and weakness. Certain stock symbols as John bull Uncle Sam. The Red Bear, The land of rising sun or Swastika etc. may be used to explain the point of view or the other.

Limitations of Cartoons : Cartoons may have certain limitations:

(i) Sometimes these may be wrongly interpreted and the students may get wrong impressions.

(ii) For young students it is difficult to interpret the cartoons.

(iii) The teacher if he is making use of cartoons must be extra-careful to help the students to judge and understand them.

(iv) In the beginning, the teacher may be handicapped to use them effectively.

(v) Their use make the lesson and the activity more lively and interesting.

Cartoons can be used both as a fixing device and as a teaching device.

But we must be aware ourselves against wrong impressions formed and against the stereo-type perpetuating false ideas. The teacher should correct wrong assimilation. It sometimes becomes a greatly emotionally changed media and must be used with care and courtesy.

Cartoons may be made by the students and also they may gather them from magazines, newspapers and may be arranged and kept in a folder. The Home Science teacher in particular and other teachers in general must get a good selection of cartoons to make their teaching more effective.

Projective Aids

In this type of teaching aids are included such aids as film strips, slides, opaque pictures, motion pictures etc.

Slides

It is a popular visual-aids for the teaching of Home Science. They can easily be prepared and preserved and can be used several times. The teacher can enlarge the pictures on the slides to any desired size by projecting them on the screen. They facilitate for discussion and note taking.

In those cases where slides can not be used conveniently we can make use of film strips. A film-strip contains a series of still pictures about 24 to 48 frames arranged in sequence.

The film-strip combines certain diagrams and situations in a proper sequence. The ideas are beautifully presented before the students. However, the teacher should plan the use of film strips and should see for herself before using them for the pupils. The teacher should know the details and other points that have to be emphasised.

Advantages of Projective Aids

(i) Film strips can give new colour and attraction to different ideas.

(ii) The image can be kept before the students as long as we desire. The diagrams or results can be shown again and again.

(iii) These do not burden the minds of the students.

(iv) These can be shown even in off hours.

(v) There is an element of novelty and motivation in projective aids. Some other projective aids and Epidiascope, Magic lantern etc.

Epidiascope

Unless the slides are prepared, the object cannot be projected in a magic frames. To remove such defect Epidiascope is used. Any picture, diagram, map or sketch, photographed specimen or small object can be projected straight way. No slides are needed. Any page from the book, any printed sheets can be very conveniently projected. But it cannot be manipulated without electricity. It is an improvement on the magic lantern.

The Epidiascope can be used as a lantern (diascope) for the projection of slides and also as an episcope for taking projection of three dimensional illustrations or objects placed in horizontal plane at its base.

The main advantage of epidiascope projection is that the original colours of the diagram, pictures, photo etc. are reproduced. We can keep the projected material on the board for any length of time.

While using it as an educational aid it may be kept in mind that epidiascope projections are not very long and all efforts be made to keep to minimum the number of illustrations. It helps to avoid any intermixing of images at the end of the lesson.

Magic Lantern

A magic lantern is an optical device used to project picture on the screen. In case the object (on slide) is very small then magnified picture of object can be projected on the screen.

Every school cannot afford to have a projector, then a magic lantern which is not costly is a good substitute. It can be conveniently improvised and what matters is the preparation of the slides. Some simple slides can be easily made by the teacher or the students if they are given a little training to do so. Lantern slides covered with thin coating of transparent gum, provide suitable surface for coloured inks. We may write on the glass-slide with photographic titling ink. A magnified object on the screen can be better explained to the students as a class, then the tiny object picture or sketch, etc. handled by the teacher. Magic lantern has tremendous educative potentialities. But there must be some orderly procedure. The following four steps are necessary:

Preparation: Preparation on the part of the teacher to give comments on the subjects projected and also prepares the students to receive the new knowledge. Some things before hand must be told to the students about what they are going to see. Its value lies in the psychological law of readiness.

Presentation: When the slides are projected, a running commentary or explanation should be given by the teacher. This may clear some of the vague ideas of the students, as well as fix their attention on important aspects of the material presented.

Discussion: After the show is over, the teacher and the pupils should discuss about the material presented. It should be a co-operative affair. Pupils should be encouraged to express themselves.

Application: It depends on the nature of the slides projected. If it was for information sake only, the knowledge gained may be applied in asking allied question from the students.

Models

A model is the replica of object. By the help of this one can reproduce the original. Broadly speaking any recognisable imitation of a real object may be taken as a model. A model may be smaller or large in size according to the need. Models prepared by the students have a great educative value. It gives an opportunity for self-expression. In the teaching of Home Sciences models like doll of a new born baby, domesticated animals, money, market in different ages, models of human dwellings, utensils, ornaments, etc., can be prepared for the class-room use.

Graphs

Graph is nothing but a device for effective and accurate representation of quantitative data for showing comparison trends developments and relationships. Statistical data can be shown in an interesting manner by the help of graph. The graphs are used to show the parts of family expenditure on different heads.

Suspense Charts

Such charts have many different horizontal panels and are used as an effective trick to add interest to the talk by the teacher. In such a chart each panel stresses as certain point and it is stressed by the teacher at proper time as her talk progresses.

Posters

They are the picture of people and objects. They represent certain ideas in the symbolic language. They are used as teaching aids e.g., the educators of family planning make use of poster depicts such ideas as "we are two" and "we have two", "small family is a happy family".

Radio

In modern times, radio forms an important teaching aid. It serves the purposes of quick education. It also provides the pupils with opportunities to listen to the talks by experts in their fields. It promotes in pupils a wider understanding of themselves, their surroundings. It develops in them the habit of observation. It presents an integrated picture and idea contained in a topic.

A good school broadcast can give the teacher, through its subject matter, the freshness of its presentation, and the new technique of studio production. It offers immense scope for economic and effectiveness of teaching effort. One of the most significant aspect of broadcast is that it combines the qualities both speech and writing. The radio uses expression and sentence structures which are more easily comprehensible. Being primarily concerned with spoken word, the radio breathes life into the dead words of written materials.

No doubt, the listener does not see the speaker in his physical form. But the voice has a way of conveying the impression of personality. From the voice the listener observes whether the speaker is serious or not while delivering the topic in Home Science.

Many people fear and suspect that school broadcast does not follow the Home Science syllabus fully. But syllabus is not the end in itself. It is a means to enable the students to know more and to grow to fullness. They give certain skill and offer them disciplines so whether, the school broadcast programme strictly follows the syllabus topic by topic or not, they provide some new information, rearrange the content in a new pattern and enables the students of Home Science to see the events in clearer perspective.

In fact, the school broadcasts can, in the hands of a thoughtful teacher, become a labour-saving and time-saving device. It helps in correlation in Home Science. Therefore, the radio programmes to school should not be subject-centered. They should rather be life-centered. They should at any rate set up standards of speech and performances for students and teachers alike. If the Home Science teacher keeps contact with the school broadcast programmes, she can make Home Science an interesting subject. Therefore, the school broadcast programme should be very effectively.

Gramophone

Gramophone may be put to a variety of uses to teach pronunciation and instruction in speech, to inculcate a love of music for physical drill proposes, or for recitation of poems, etc. The value of the gramophone is the greatest in the teaching of music, language and literary appreciation and in speech training. The advantage of the record is that like the film strip, it can be specially selected to illustrate a particular point. It can be stopped or started at any point in building up the lesson and thus is under the control of the teacher. Every school must have a set of lingua-phone records in order to teach language correctly. Gramophone with some good records is not a costly thing. Every school can afford to buy it. A good collection of educational records in an essential point records of famous speeches by national leaders, great men, etc, can be heard on the gramophone. The school dramatic club may utilize the gramophone for several purposes for songs, dancing and other items children are interested in music, songs and tunes. They learn incidentally in the teaching material and accompanied by teacher can listen to a record before, prepare a plan for its use, and gather supplementary material to give his own comments on it, and thus to add to the information.

Tape Recorder

A good phonograph should be regarded as an almost indispensable adjunct of a well-equipped school. It may be used in a variety of ways. The modern recording comes in two types.

(1) Engraved on a disk.

(2) Magnetised on tape.

The disks vary in speed and the faster these turn, i.e., more r.p.m's (revolution per minute), the less will be amount of recorded materials. Disks play at 78.48 and 33 3 r.p.m. and the diameter range from 7 to 16 inches. The recording done on a magnetised tape in different in its playback equipment. It cannot be used with disks.

A phonograph is an instrument by means of which sound can be permanently registered and afterwards mechanically reproduced. Our purposes in recording may be many.

Acquisition of Skills

(a) The tape-recorder may record voices of students for speech improvement. Their pronunciation and intotation may be improved upon. Records may suggest standards their musical performances and aromatic ability be improved. The students feel a thrill of joy to hear their own sounds.

(b) It can also be used for vocal and instrumental music. The child can be made conscious of the need for improvement. It also enables him to judge his progress. Recorded data can bring realism into the class-room. The recorded voices of eminent men on certain topics may be used as a living text.

If the school is equipped with a recording machine, it can very usefully prepare its own records. Educational broadcasts and speeches may be transcribed from the radio and plays and music performances may be recorded. In addition to its direct value, such type of recording may have an indirect value as well. When some recorded commentary is needed to a company slides or film-strips the recording can be very useful help.

Audio-Visual Aids

Television

The television can also be used in teaching Home Science. Expert teachers in Home Science can deliver lessons and dramas can also be acted on it. It is just an improvement on the radio programme. It can instruct the ear and catch the eyes of the pupils. Television is "the blackboard dramatised, the picture brought to life". It stimulates the students to learn more.

In television programme, the teacher should only be a supervisor. The topic presented by the television teacher should be enriched by the class-room teacher. This programme supplements the teaching in the class-room.

We should bear in mind the Audio-visual aids in Home Science are not a panacea for our all ills. They are also not a poison. They have merits and demerits too, it is the responsibility of the teacher to use them effectively to achieve better results. By the help of Audio-visual aids, we catch the visual memory, and appeal the auditory memory of the students. In India, we are not in a position, so far to use these Audio-visual aids for want of funds. Therefore, attempts should be made to devise similar and cheaper aids which our schools can afford to purchase and prepare by the help of the students.

Films

Films are audio-visual-aids that enable the child to see things and hear them. It provides meaningful experiences through motion pictures. It promotes greater understanding and motivation. Documentary films, instructional films, news reels and even some commercial films with educative volume can be shown to pupils to make the teaching of Home Science lively, interesting and effective.

Effective use of films needs certain amount of teaching skill and experiences. Therefore, teacher should know how to show a particular film. He should plan it before hand and should prepare notes also.

Conditions for the successful use of Audio-visual Aids in Teaching English : Audio-visual aids are nothing, but means to end. Its success depends upon the following conditions:

(i) Audio-visual aids should be selected on the basis of criteria set up in terms of the purposes of instruction, and the needs of pupils.

(ii) The teacher should try to present accurate and authentic aids.

(iii) Unless the aids are properly explained by the teacher, they never become effective. Hence, they should be deliberately utilised for the teaching purpose and should be explained properly.

(iv) For the successful use of the aids, the teacher should come prepared to the class. He should use them exactly when they are required to be used.

(v) There should be scope for the participation of the pupils in the preparation and presentation of the audio-visual aids.

(vi) Economic use of time is another essential condition for the successful use the aids. Hence, proper selection of aids should be done.

(vii) While selecting aids, the stage of mental development of the children should be taken into consideration. They should be suitable to the age, intelligence and experience of the students of particular class.

(viii) Over-use aids should be avoided. It will reduce the value of novelty of the aids.

(ix) While using the aid., the teacher should consider and evaluate the pupil's ability and interest, their attitude participation and the general atmosphere of the class-room.

(x) The aids should be used at such times and ways that learning is facilitated.

(xi) Intelligent planning is required in their production and use.

(xii) The effectiveness of audio-visual aids depends upon the skill of the user.

(xiii) The teaching aids should be prepared under favourable conditions. All the students should be able to hear and see comfortably.

(xiv) Appropriate aids should be prepared for the students.

"It should be borne in mind that audio-visual aids including television which is still in infancy are neither a panacea nor a poison." They have both dark side and bright-side. It is the responsibility of the teacher to select them properly and use effectively to make his language teaching effective, lively and interesting.

Suggestions for Effective Use

These aids serve their purpose best only when these are rightly used. Following suggestions are to be kept in mind while making use of these aids:

(i) The aid should serve some useful purpose. Aid should not be used just for the sake of using an aid. Rather it should help in teaching a particular lesson. The teacher should be clear about the purpose for which he is using the aid.

(ii) The aid should be selected according to the general interests, abilities of the pupils.

(iii) The size of the aid should be neither too large nor too small. It should be clearly visible to the students.

(iv) Aid should be used only at the right moment. If it is meant for introduction of the lesson, it should be shown at the proper time. Aid used at the wrong time may prove harmful.

(v) If a number of aids are to be used, then every aid must be used at the proper time and not in a haphazard manner. The systematic display gives good results.

(vi) The aid should be kept before the students as long as it serves some purpose. It should be removed when it has served its purpose.

(vii) While using aids teacher should always bear in mind that teaching aids are only means and not an end.

Problems in the Use

While various teaching aids are becoming more and more popular day by day, there are still some problems to the faced and solved. Some of these are:

Apathy of Teachers. The teachers are yet to be convinced that teaching with words alone is very tedious, wasteful and ineffective.

Indifference of Students. The judicious use of aids arouses interest but when used without a definite purpose they lose their significance and importance.

Ineffectiveness of the Aids. In the absense of proper planning and lethargy of the teacher and without proper preparation, correct presentation, appropriate application and discussion and the essential follow up work, the aids have not proved their usefulness. A film like a good lesson has various steps Preparation, Presentation, Application and Discussion.

Financial Hurdles. The central and state governments have set up Boards of Audio-visual Education and have chalked out interesting programmes for the popularisation of teaching aids but the lack of finance is not enabling them to do their best.

Abscence of Electricity. Most of the projectors can not work without electricity and so are not utilised properly.

Lack of Facility for Training. More and more training colleges or specialised agencies should be opened to train teachers and workers in the use and usefulness of these aids.

Lack of Coordination between Central and State Governments. Good film libraries, museums of audio-visual education, fixed and mobile exhibitions and educational rules can be organised only if there is full coordination between state government and centre.

Language Difficulty. Most films are in English. It is desirable to have these in Hindi and other Indians languages.

Not Catering to Local Needs. No attention is paid in the production of audio-visual aids to the sociological, psychological and pedagological factors.

Improper Selection of Films. Generally the films are not selected in accordance with the needs of a class.

Conclusion

Today the problem is not whether audio-visual aids should have a place in education. This has been recognised long ago. The problem now is that of extending the benefits of these aids to all teachers and all children. The future could be bright if there is a proper planning as the part of the government and coordination between producers, teachers and students.

India is a country with limited resources. It is not expected to have large collection of such material aids. The teacher has to make best possible use of such aids available to them. While using such aids teacher should keep in mind the psychological requirements of the students.

QUESTIONS

1. "A teaching aid, however, good it may be, cannot replace teacher." Discuss.
2. What are audio-visual aids? How far they are useful for teaching of Home Science?
3. Discuss the educational value of
   - (i) Charts, diagrams, pictures etc.
   - (ii) Radio
   - (iii) Computers
   - (iv) Television
   - (v) Field-trips
   - (vi) Films.

4. Write short notes on

   (i) Flannel Board

   (ii) Overhead Projector

   (iii) Slide Projector.

5. "Home-task is not required for the children." Support your answer with suitable examples. What visual aids can you use to teach the child at home?

6. Comment on role of audio-visual aids in teaching Home Science.

7. Write short notes on Home-Task.

8. Define Audio-Visual Aids. Write about different auditory aids.

9. What is the role of aids in teaching? What points should be kept in mind while giving Home-Assignments?

10. How are the text-books helpful in teaching? Which points would you consider while selecting Home Science text books?

11. What are field trips? How are they organized?

10

The Library

One of the important recommendations by the Secondary Education Commission was that every school should have subject libraries which are under the charge of subject teacher. It was felt that subject teacher can enrich their teaching making use of small collection of books on their own subjects. The need for subject library is utmost. A Home Science library should be an essential part of each school which undertakes Home Science teaching.

In the modern school systems library services has got wide recognition. A good library is a *sine qua non* of good teaching and effective learning. It is an integral part of the school.

The Need

An explosion has occurred in scientific knowledge in recent past and teachers of Home Science find it difficult to keep themselves equipped with the newest knowledge in the subject. For acquainting himself with such a knowledge he needs a good library from where he can find out the latest and new books to update his knowledge. He can then recommend some books to his students and may encourage them to acquire the habit of extending and supplementing their knowledge by making proper use of the library. A subject library can thus serve as a wonderful teaching aid. By extra-books students can get a good deal of general knowledge which he may not get if he depends entirely on the class-room teaching.

In the school, our aim is not merely to prepare pupils for the examinations, the objectives of school education are to widen the outlook of the students, to instil in them a love of extra reading. A textbook conveys knowledge and information in some specific way. A growing and developing learner craves for wider and extensive contacts with others, their writings and their saying. He does not like to remain confined to the length and breath of a textbook knowledge, class room teaching and examination-oriented teaching. To take him out of this narrow grooves the keen need is felt for some adequate device.

With the above in mind, it was felt that some steps are urgently, required to be taken for paying special attention to widen the intellectual horizon of the students of Home Science and to provide them some facilities so that they may read beyond their examinations and the prescribed syllabus. In addition to it, various other pursuits of co-curricular activities, many academic studies, group work and individual work and assignments postulate the existence of a good library service. A library is to act as the educational hub of all school activities.

The Organisation

Though a well equipped subject library under the charge of subject teacher is desirable yet a Home Science library under the charge of Home Science teacher can serve the purpose of all Home Science subjects. Such a library be set up preferably in a small room or in a corner of the Home Science laboratory where some shelves or almirahs be reserved for storing the library books. The Home Science teacher can equip the library depending on the availability of funds and accommodation for the purpose. For setting up rich library with limited funds, it is necessary that Home Science teacher is very thoroughly acquainted with the latest and good books available as the subject. For building up a good Home Science library teacher should select for the library only such books which cover wide range of topics. These should be the books that deal with topics in cooking, laundering, nature study, environment, ecology, pollution etc. Books on romance of Home Science, engineering, scientific discoveries and inventions, quiz, projects, fun in Home Science etc. must also find a place in Home Science library. Home Science library should also have some books on the lives and achievements of some great scientist and some books dealing with hobbies like photography, fashion and designs etc. Some standard reference books and books on methods of teaching Home Science be also purchased for school library.

The selection of books is a difficult task and Home Science teachers can solve it by making use of fairly exhaustive list of books available from various publishers. For list of such books he can also seek guidance and help from N.B.T. (National Book Trust) of India, NCERT and other such organisations as SCERT of their state. Home Science teacher should also read reviews of books published in some good journals for schools e.g. School science review, popular science and industry etc.

Recommendations of All India Seminar

Important recommendations about science library as made by All India seminar on the Teaching of Science are as under:

(i) Each school should have a separate science library.

(ii) Science books of general interest be stored in the school library.

(iii) A separate section be allocated in science library for reference books. Reference books are for use by teacher' as also by students but these should not be ordinarily issued for home use.

(iv) Books on methods of teaching science be stored in a separate section in science library and these are meant for use of science teacher.

(v) Science teacher be asked to become incharge of science library. He may be assisted in his library work by a small committee of students.

(vi) Teachers should take some measures to encourage love for library books amongst his students. Teacher can ask the students to prepare a brief review of the books read by them and some of these reviews considered good be published in science magazine and science bulletins.

(vii) A cross reference index be prepared in which teacher and students indicate briefly the information contained in the book ready by them. Such an information may be provided under the relevant heads and a proper use be made of this index for guiding the students in their reading.

(viii) Complete sets of various text books should be available in school library.

(ix) A few laboratory manuals must also be available in school library.

Aims to be Achieved

By the proper use of library, it is expected to achieve the following aims:

(i) Encourage reading habit in pupils.

(ii) To develop the ability to learn, from books, in the students, if left to themselves.

(iii) Break the rigidity of time-table that isolates one subject from the other.

(iv) To provide better opportunities to the students for social training.

Advantages of Library

We have a number of advantages that accrue from an efficient library service. The library proves to be instrumental in putting progressive methods of teaching into practice. It supplements the knowledge learnt in the class-room. No single book can be comprehensive in all its details. Extra reading is needed to make it complete. The library may develop in the students habits of supplementary reading. It incidentally educates them for leisure. The library, if properly equipped and intelligently used and service well organised, can do a lot of benefit to the school population. A library is not merely a collection of books and its advantages go far beyond of exerting some cultural influence on the child through the reading material.

Equipment for Library

The library should be housed in an attractive place that is well ventilated and well furnished, homely comfortable and workman like. The furniture, tables, chairs, catalogue stands, stacks and book shelves should be designed to provide an artistic effect and functional efficiency. There should be proper selection of books, journals, periodicals and newspapers. A small library committee may be constituted to recommend the purchase of books on different subjects teachers or the committee must be genuinely interested in the selection of the books. They may consult reviews catalogues from standard publishers as Oxford University Press Macmillan, McGraw Hills, Longman, Indian Press Ltd. Allahabad University publisher Jallandhar and Atma Ram and Sons Delhi etc. may write to training colleges for guidance. The teachers may visit book shops for selection of books. Books selected should be according to the interests and tastes of the students. There must be a separate library room. If the space in a school does not allow this it may be turned into library-cum-reading room and may be housed in the hall. The practice of placing book shelves here and there in the class-rooms should be discouraged. The area of the library may vary from 600 sq ft. to 960 sq. ft with attached reading rooms. The library should have only one door for entrance as well as for exit. That leads to proper control on the readers.

Library Service

Every school should have a fulltime librarian. The teacher in charge of library should possesses a training in library science. In the library, there should be different sections. But in each section the needs of the peoples of different intellectual capacity and attainments must be kept in mind. There is also the felt need to have a teacher's section in the library. Teacher's also need to replenish their knowledge once learnt in training colleges. Books on various aspects of Home Science should also find a proper representation in teacher's section. Textbooks, reference books, magazines, Newspapers, supplementary reading etc. should be kept in the library.

Cataloguing

The catalogue interprets the classification system of a library to the teacher. All the books may be listed three times according to the authors the title or the subject. It is through the catalogue that one can easily locate any book. It can also tell one the number of volumes the library contains on a particular subject. The catalogue may be according to the alphabetical order of the subjects or it may be a classified catalogue following Dewey's system card index may be maintained.

Class Library

In addition to the general library, there may be class libraries for each class. The class teacher may be incharge of each class library meant for a particular class. It should be wholly at his disposal. He should issue the books to his class from the class-library occasionally. The class-library may function as the tributary of the one general library and should be supplemented by books down from the general library. The class library may have sets of different books properly selected. The pupils may draw books from the class libraries according to a set programme. If the class libraries function properly the working load on the general library will be lightened and the library service will be more effective.

Subject Libraries

It is desirable to have subject libraries, particularly in the high classes. The subject teacher may be the incharge of subject library. If the teacher takes pains to build good library services, he can enrich this section through collections of good books on their subjects. The subject libraries should not be confined merely to the stocking of text-books. Advanced works and reference books on the subject should find a suitable place in them. Pupils should be guided to make use of subject libraries.

If library service is to function efficiently the Head master should see that there is provision in the Time-Table, when different classes can go to the reading room and study also that books are regularly issued to the students. New books, properly selected are added to the library each year. Attention of the students may be drawn to the new books added to the library their title pages, etc., with brief comments may be displayed at the Notice Board. Book exhibitions may be arranged from time to time.

For any library to act as the intellectual life of a school it should be well-planned and systematically organised.

The prevailing conditions in most of the schools are not encouraging and a proper attention should be paid for improvement in our school libraries.

QUESTIONS

1. What are the advantages of a Library ?
2. What are subject liabraries ?

11

Time-Table

Time-table is a form of planning the time. It enables a person to remain disciplined in his life. It is required to accomplish work efficiently and successfully. The school time-table is a means to organise the school work methodically.

H.G. Stead's View, "It is the time-table that supplies the frame work within which his work of the school proceeds. It is the instrument through which the purpose of the school is to function."

Mohiyuddin's View, "A time-table is said to be the second school clock. It shows the hours during which school work is done, what work is to be done during each period of the school-day and in each class, the room in which the work is to be done and the teacher to be in-charge of that work."

Dr. Jaswant Singh's View, "The schedule is spark plug of the school which sets into motion its various activities and programmes."

Thus it can be concluded that time-table is a mirror which reflects the entire educational plan of the school. It is a kind of frame work for various school activities. It shows a systematic and pre-planned scheme of work to be done by the students and the teachers of various classes and sections. It includes all the subjects of studies and other educational activities showing the days and time allotted to them. In the time-table time is allotted for morning assembly, hours of study, lunch break, roll call, library, craft, community service, games, physical exercise and other activities and is extended even after the school hours. A proper time-table includes the home task also.

Need of the School Time-table

A good time-table is must for the efficient functioning of the school. The Education has its main aim the all round development of the child. This is achieved through the school curriculum which consists of a number of subjects, activities and programmes. The importance of time- table can be summarised as under

Smooth and Orderly Work: The school time-table ensures smooth, orderly and systematic work. The teacher and students know what is to be done, when and where to be done. The students know the subjects that they are going to read in different periods and also the teachers who will teach these subjects. It develops a methodical attitude towards both in teachers and students. It helps in the placement of right persons, at right places, at the right time and in the right manner. It saves the teacher and students from unnecessary worries and tensions.

Ensures Proper Distribution of Work-load: Time-table ensures that the work is distributed evenly among the students. It helps in avoiding the allotment of too much or too less work to one teacher. While going through the time table the head of the institute gets the chance to see the periods allotted to each teacher. This helps him to balance the teaching load of the teachers. Moreover the specific subjects are assigned to those teachers only in which they are efficient. It removes many grudges, conflicts or complaints which are bound to arise. It helps in the efficient working of the teacher and they feel their responsibility.

Adjustment according to the requirements of Pupils: School time-table is adjusted according to the physiological and psychological needs of the students. Periods are so adjusted that the more difficult subjects are in the morning time when students are not tired and have more of concentration. The subjects like crafts, music, drawing etc. are kept in the later periods when the students are tired and start loosing their concentration. At this time interesting and light subjects keep children engrosed in their work. Intervals of rest and recreation are also provided in the school time-table. Number of periods to a particular subject are also provided keeping in mind the difficulty of the subject.

Avoids Wastage of Time and Energy: Planned work is helpful in preventing wastage of time and energy. When the students and teachers know their specific task at the right time and in the right manner it becomes just a routine work to do a specified task at the right time and in the right manner and avoid burden on them.

Maintenance of Discipline: Time-table is so framed to keep the students busy. Thus they do not get the time for creating indiscipline. Students energy is directed in the proper direction and their minds are kept occupied when a teacher is on leave, the, headmaster while going through the time table can decide which teacher to send in that class so that the students do not make noise and roam about. A good time-table creates harmony and smoothness in the various activities of the school and there is no over-lapping of their function. In this way school functions orderly. In the absence of time-table school work will become chaos and confusion. It can lead to unnecessary conflicts.

Second School Clock: Time-table works like a second time clock which has written record of periods, intervals of rest etc. It clearly specifies what is to be done, when, where and whom to do.

Caters to Needs: A proper time-table is planned according to the requirements of the students. The work is planned according to their physical, mental, social and psychological needs. Psychological factors like interests, fatigue, preferred activities, freshness of body and mind should be considered while planning time-table. When the children are satisfied they work in a peaceful and happy way.

Develops Good Habits: A good time-table helps in developing a number of good habits like orderliness, regularity, punctuality, hard work, value of discipline and steadiness of purpose among students as well as teachers. Students become responsible persons. A sense of devotion to duty is developed. It prevents slackness and negligence.

Ensures Regular and Uniform Progress: The good time-table ensures regular and uniform progress in various subjects and in the organisation of co-curricular activities. It prevents over emphasis or negligence of a particular subject. If time table is defective, regular progress is not possible in different subjects.

Ensures Realisation of School Objectives: Aims and purposes of the school can be achieved through the proper time-table. If a school wants to propagate a particular idea, philosophy or religion or wants to emphasise moral education, sports and so on, time table provides necessary arrangement in the direction.

To summarise, school time-table is very significant part of school life for the smooth, orderly and efficient working of the institute, for preventing wastage of time and energy, for regulating the working habits, for developing good habits of work and recreation, for organising the co-curricular activities, for realising the school objectives, for reflecting the philosophy of school and for following the departmental instructions regarding. the education of school children.

The Advantages

Time-table is essential for every school. It has the following advantages

(i) Time-table ensures proper distribution of work among the teachers.

(ii) It helps in regularity and uniformity of school work.

(iii) Every subject or activity is given due importance.

(iv) It prevents wastage of time and energy.

(v) It develops the habit of discipline and punctuality.

(vi) It helps in overall development of the child.

(vii) It helps in smooth functioning of the school.

(viii) It keeps teachers and students busy and prevents indiscipline.

(ix) Time-table helps teachers to prepare the work before hand.

(x) It helps to minimise the fatigue and boredom of students and teachers.

(xi) It meets the requirements of school and students. In this way it helps in smooth functioning of the institution.

Various Types

The different types of time-table are as follows

General Time-table: It is consolidated time-table which includes the working of the whole school. It is time table of all classes, teachers and students. It includes the time-table of different wings and groups. This time-table gives the whole picture of the work of the school. A copy of this time-table is kept in the headmaster's office so that he knows the functioning of each wing of the school.

Class-Time-table: This time-table deals with the particular class or section. It shows the programme of a particular class. It is kept in the class-room so that the teacher in-charge knows the programme of the class and the class works according to its own class time-table.

Time-table for Games and Other Activities: This is time-table to specify the duration, place etc. of the games and other activities. A copy of this time-table is kept by the teacher in-charge of games and in-charge of co-curricular activities.

Time-table for Home Work: Home-work should be planned before hand so that its motives and purposes are not lost. For this, home work time-table is prepared. Different subject teachers teaching a particular class sit together towards the week-end and plan next week's home work to be given to the class.

Teacher's Time-table: This type of time-table is prepared for the convenience of teachers and the principal. From this principal keeps the knowledge when and where a teacher is busy or free. It also helps the principle to send a teacher to a class which is free due to the absence of its teacher. A copy of this time-table is kept in the staff room and another copy by the head of the institution.

Subject Time-table: This time-table is prepared subjectwise and class wise. It indicates which subject is taught in a particular class at a particular time.

All these time-tables are necessary for the efficient functioning of the school.

QUESTIONS

1. What points will you keep in mind while framing the time-table of your school?

2. What is the need of planning school time-table?

3. How many types of time-tables are planned in the school?

12

The Laboratory

No course in Home Science can be considered as complete without including some practical work in it. The practical work is to be carried out by individual in a Home Science laboratory. At school stage practical work is even more important because of the fact that we 'learn by doing'. Practical class-room experiments help in broadening pupil's experience and develop initiative, resourcefulness and cooperation. Because of the above reasons, practical work forms a prominent feature in any Home Science course.

For every subject a separate room is essential. For teaching literary subjects ordinary rooms may serve the purpose but for teaching of subjects like Home Science a separate room is essential. Because of financial difficulties it is not possible for every school to have a separate Home Science room but it is desirable to have it and equip it with suitable material required for teaching of Home

Science. In the absence of a separate Home Science room the teacher will not get a congenial atmosphere which is quite essential for teaching of Home Science. Like any other science laboratory, workshop or laboratory of Home Science creates a congenial atmosphere and stimulates the imagination of students and gives them the inspiration.

Location of Home Science Room

Laboratory is a spacious room wherein a group of students carry out their practicals. The work of designing and building a Home Science room (laboratory and lecturer room) is that of the architect but Home Science teacher should collaborate with the architect in planning for what is best from the educational point of view.

The Home Science room may be located on any floor of the train building. Following factors may be considered while planning the room. If possible it be put up on the first floor of the main building and preferably near the entrance-various factors to be considered while planning a Home Science room as a separate unit:

(i) Curriculum,

(ii) Type of class organisation,

(iii) Number and size of the class,

(iv) The number of periods the room is likely to be occupied,

(v) Various other uses to which this room is likely to be used,

(vi) Provision of future expansion,

(vii) Other facilities available in school, and

(viii) Financial position etc.

Keeping in view the above points, it can easily be concluded that such a room will be different from the ordinary class-room. The minimum requirement for such a room are as follows:

It is generally two times the size of an ordinary class-room. It is so because for covering different areas of the curriculum adequate space and equipment have to be provided.

It is planned in such a way as to have a flexible arrangement of equipment and materials.

It should look attractive and should give a home like appearance.

It should be provided with safe and sanitary conditions.

Adequate storage facilities be provided in it.

It should be equipped with equipment and furnishing that can be easily looked after with minimum effort.

Adequate provision of lighting be provided and should also be provided with good ventilation.

Its walls should be painted with colours that give pleasant appearance.

Sufficient water be supplied to the room by making good provisions for water supply.

Some space be reserved for certain special purposes such as home management and clothing.

Work Centres

It is the duty of the Home Science teacher to plan different type of work centres so as to provide for all the activities included in the Home Science curriculum. If possible, a work centre may be used to carry out more than one activity. Some of the activities for which work centres may be planned are listed below:

(i) Arranging and carrying for a bed-room. Space for providing experiences in planning, arranging and caring for different rooms.

(ii) Planning and discussion by small groups, tables, chairs, blackboard for discussion.

(iii) Cupboards for books and other articles prepared by the students.

(iv) Preparing and serving meals-fire places, work spaces, home kitchen equipment, utensils, linen, cutery and provision for care and disposal of garbage.

(v) Selecting and constructing clothing-sewing machines, tables and chairs, irons, and ironing boards space for fitting garments, mirror and sewing kits.

(vi) For teaching child development, operating a nursery school.

(vii) A sick-room.

(viii) Teacher's place. It is a work centre provided with desks, files etc.

(ix) Laundering sinks, buckets etc.

(x) Special activity such as flower arrangement, refinishing furniture and handicrafts.

(xi) Home furnishing and house care living dinning centre for experience in hospitability, home decoration etc.

Storage Space

In the space meant for storage the provision be made for the storage of the following items:

Foods, Nutrition and Cookery

(i) Shelves for dishes, utensils and equipment not in daily use.

(ii) Meat-safe.

(iii) Cupboards for kitchen linen.

(iv) Place for crockery, cutlery and other serving dishes.

Textiles, Clothing and Laundry

(i) Storage space for irons, pressing clothes, ironing boards.

(ii) Soaps and supplies for stain removal.

(iii) Cup-boards for storing materials replaced by the students:

(iv) Space for hanging garments that have been switched by the students.

Space for Keeping Home Nursing and First-aid Equipment

Child Development and Mother-Craft

(i) Storage space for toys, books and other material used for teaching child development.

(ii) Supplies and equipments used for house cleaning.

(iii) Storage for supplies for teaching, care of babies, bathing, feeding and dressing.

Home Management and Care House

(i) Storage for supplies and equipment for house cleaning.

(ii) Space for articles to be used in making home attractive such as vases for flowers, mats etc.

(iii) Equipment and supplies and for repairing and renovating furniture and for making curtains, covers and drapperies etc.

Additional Storage Facilities

Provision should be made for the following :

(i) Charts, old magazines and other teaching materials.

(ii) Books and other personal belongings of the students.

(iii) Books, bulletins and other reference materials.

(iv) Miscellaneous supplies such as textiles, paper, pins, scissors, needles etc.

Equipments and Furnishing

While providing for equipments and furnishings, the following points be taken into consideration:

(i) Promoting flexibility in use and arrangement.

(ii) Representing good applications of art principles.

(iii) Strength and durability of the articles.

(iv) Variation in type and quality, which are needed in teaching.

(v) Standard of living of the community.

(vi) Equipments should be such as can provide meaningful experiences.

A Home Science room should be just like a home in the community. It is essential to take into considerations the income level of the community. With the changing standards in the society, the Home Science department should improve.

Managing the Department

An ideal Home Science department is just like home in the community. It is a living center, a work center and social centre. At both places i. e. (home and school) the same basic principles of management are applicable but there is some difference in the details of their use and their applications. This difference arises due to the fact, the home is in use all the 24 hours and its management is in the hands of the parents.

One of the most important things to be kept in mind for managing the Home Science department is that sufficient care is taken for the equipment to be kept in the department.

It is also essential that it should be kept neat, clean and tidy. For this, cleaning must be done daily. All possible efforts be made to make the appearance of the room attractive.

All the records and registers kept in the department must always be maintained properly and should be updated every day. It is also desirable to keep the supplies of the department in such a manner that they are easily accessible.

Up-keep and Managing House Keeping

Maintenance of proper discipline in the Home Science department is a must for up-keeping and managing house-keeping.

All the articles of the department be kept in an orderly manner at some convenient places. It helps the students to develop the essential habits and attitudes for the clean and well-ordered home. All the work in the department be completed in a business-like manner. The maintenance of proper records be clearly explained to the students. They should also be taught the business methods in handling the purchases of supplies, furnitures and equipments. All-out efforts be made to create a home-like atmosphere in the department. At all stages, students should learn how to develop cooperation in living together.

QUESTIONS

1. What is a work centre ?
2. How the department is managed ?

13

Measurement and Evaluation

Once a teacher has a clear idea of what she will teach and how she will teach it, she is concerned with knowing to what extent children learn from her lessons. This chapter will deal with specific procedures for evaluation the effectiveness of Home Science teaching-learning.

Evaluation is a continuous process which is an integral part of teaching. It is not merely a test at the end of Home Science lesson or unit. Instead, evaluation goes on constantly during lessons and units and is clearly related to the teacher's goal and points of view on Home Science teaching.

Besides being a continuous experience, evaluation is cumulative. A cumulative record should be kept for all children. If such a record is available then his mathematics exposure can be quickly and easily seen.

The recent trends in learning and evaluation link them to behavioural objectives. According to a behaviourist psychology learning is defined as a charge in the behaviour of an individual that can be described in terms of observable and measurable performance. The changes in behaviour are affected by providing experiences and thorough teaching.

The test efficiency of teaching, to judge the progress of students and to discover their achievements and evaluate the whole school system, we require some sort of measuring tools. These tools are tests or examinations. Tests are essential to grade and rank pupils, however, if evaluation is used merely to indicate areas of science of which children have been exposed or for classifying and categorizing students, a great value is lost. The same loss occurs if evaluation is interpreted only as arriving at numerical or alphabetical ratings for report cards. In this way, much of the positive use of evaluation as a means of teaching and learning could be destroyed.

Effective instructional planning and evaluation of students performance have always stressed on the statement of instructional objectives so that they are of great help to the student. According to Muller, an instructionally usable objective must state the intended outcome in terms of the terminal behaviour of students. Terminal behaviour here means the behaviour of students after the class room instruction and evaluation is possible if the learning outcomes are carefully specified. By combining continuous evaluation with immediate application of what has been learned, the teacher can provide for:

(i) The stimulation of students who learn rapidly to greater growth towards goals by application of advanced works.

(ii) The identification of specific weaknesses and difficulties in functional understanding (concepts, principles, generalization) and the needed re-teaching of varied activities skills or problems solving ability, and

(iii) The clarification, modification or complete alternation of the goals as needed for the unit.

Evaluation, teaching and learning are the three corners of the education system. Evaluation is concerned with finding out how far students have learned as a consequence of teaching. There are two kinds of evaluation depending upon whether the comparison of students is made with some absolute performance standard or with other students of a given group. These are known as criterion reference evaluation and norm referenced evaluation.

Criterion-reference Evaluation

It assesses the students, performance in terms of a specified performance standard or criterion without any mention of the performance levels of the other students of the group. This evaluation method is related to mastery and development test.

Norm-reference Evaluation

It assesses the students, performance relative to other students of the group. Students are awarded marks and relative ranks in this method of evaluation.

Purpose of Evaluation

In Mathematics evaluation is needed for the purposes noted below:

(i) For determining the teaching learning process.

(ii) For revising curriculum.

(iii) To provide an objective basis for reporting progress of students.

(iv) For securing effective cooperation from the parents and the community.

(v) For determining the policies of promotion,

(vi) To provide suitable guidance to pupils, on the basis of their evaluation.

Thus we find that evaluation is an essential part of the educational process. It helps in realising the goals of instruction. It points out the defects in the teaching-learning process. It also helps in ascertaining the effectiveness of the curriculum, methods and devices of teaching etc.

The Characteristics

A good test in Home Science should have the following characteristics:

Validity: The test should be valid. It should fulfill the objectives for which it is meant. If our aim is to measure the ability to understand and application of various facts then language difficulty and speed should not come in way. Thus, it should be free from defects that are likely to affect the valid results.

Reliability: The test is considered to be reliable if it gives same results every time when it is used for testing the individual's abilities under same conditions. An objective test is bound to be reliable.

The reliability of a test is affected by the following factors, thus to be reliable it should be free from:

(a) The whims of an examiner.

(b) The physical and mental condition of the student.

(c) The language of the questions-lack of clearness or any ambiguities in statements.

(d) Lack of clear-cut instructions for making.

(e) Inefficient methods of scoring.

A reliable test is not influenced by subjective conditions; it is objective.

Comprehensiveness: Any good test should be comprehensive i.e. it should assess knowledge, skills, abilities, attitudes, etc. as adequately as possible. No aspect of the curriculum should be ignored while making evaluation.

Administrability: It should be easy to administer, economical in time and money, easy to score and interpret. The directions of the test should be clear-cut. There should be answer-keys for scoring.

Capable of Maintaining the Interest of the Students: Any good test should be able to capture the interest of the students and maintain it. Thus, it should be interesting for the students. A good test is motivating for the students and stimulates their best efforts. It should be neither too easy nor too difficult. It should never be used as a means of punishment.

Diagnosticity: A good test is diagnostic. The aim of diagnosis is to analyse the difficulties of a student in a particular phase of work. The aim is to reveal reliable information concerning his weaknesses in order to overcome them by concentrated action and for remedial teaching. In this way, it would help the teacher to guide them properly and adopt remedial measures to eliminate their weak points.

Utility: A good test is useful in various way. For example, a test result may be used for improvement of teaching, may be useful to measure some desired quality/ability in the student, useful in finding out deficiencies in pupils so that remedial measures be taken up for their removal etc.

The Functions

The institution of examination exists since times immemorial. Every country has been maintaining the institution also. Examination have a number of functions to perform, some of these are as under:

(i) To test the efficiency of teachers in teaching standard of attainment of students and academic standing of the schools.

(ii) T o motivate students towards better attainment.

(iii) To provide useful information for the guidance of pupils, teacher, parents and others.

The Importance

Importance of examinations can hardly be minimised. The examination have been in existence, since times immemorial. "To close down examinations would be to give the signal for educational saturnalia." Observed Michael Sadler.

Similarly, J.C. Mathur emphasizes the value of examinations where he writes, "Even in the idealized picture of society portrayed is H. G. Wells Utopia, examinations find an important place."

The Secondary Education Commission has also observed "Nevertheless examinations and especially external examinations have a stimulating effect both on the pupils and on the teachers by providing well-defined goals and objective standards of evaluation. To the pupils, the examinations give a goal towards which he should strive and a stimulus urging him to attain that goal in a given time, thereby demanding steady and constant effort. This makes the purpose clean and the method of approach definite. He is judged by external and objective tests on which both he and others interested in him can depend. And finally, it gives him a hall mark recognised by all."

Limitations of Essay Type Examination

The present system of examination is based on essay type questions. It suffers from many a limitation. Various epithets that have been given to examinations based on essay type questions are given below:

1. A bane of educational system.
2. A begetter of rivalry and strife.
3. A blood sucker.
4. A dead hand of education.
5. A glorification of memory.
6. A growing tyranny.
7. A necessary evil.
8. A presumptuous attempt to gauge the depth of human ignorance.

9. An enemy of true education.
10. An incubus.
11. An obstacle to learning.

Main Defects

1. Element of chance.
2. Glorification of memory.
3. Heavy mental strain.
4. Lack of definite aim.
5. Lowering of educational standard.
6. Lack of objectivity.
7. Ignoring quality of character.
8. Lowering of moral standards.
9. Frustrations.

As far as the examinations in Home Science are concerned these defects can be put as under:

(i) They only test the memory of the student. Students cram up informations and produce them in examinations.

(ii) It fails to test the knowledge of entire Home Science syllabus prescribed for the students. Only a few questions are asked from selected topics.

(iii) Selection of important questions by the teachers and students is also a defect of this system of examinations.

(iv) Note-books in Home Science cut dawn the textbooks to examinations size and so the achievement of the students is not properly adjudged.

(v) It does not provide scope to bright students for their natural development.

(vi) Within limited knowledge, a student can secure very good marks.

The examinations also test the language capacity of the students. As a result, the assessment is influenced to a large extent due to the language standard of the student.

Writing about the present system (essay type) of examination, the Report of the International Commission on Examination of the New Education Fellowship opines, "The present emphasis in intellectual matter should be shifted from memory work to the cultivation of power of judgement, which implies a proper imaginative grasp and understanding of the subject. For this purpose extensive experiments should be made in the use of reference books, dictionaries etc. during the examination.

The University Education Commission (1948-49), laid great emphasis on the reform of our examination. It suggested immediate introductions of valid, reliable and objective based examinations in our country.

The Mudaliar Commission on Secondary Education (1952) recommended improvement of external examination and introduction of internal assessment and school records so as to measure fully the all round progress of the pupils. Many other committees have been set up to study and suggest changes if any in the system of examinations. They have suggested various measures and here we give a few proposals for improvement of examinations.

Some Proposals for Improvement

In order to overcome the defects of the essay type examination, we should give a combination of essay, short answer and objective type questions. Thus, we should make use of evaluation so that we can really test the realisation of instructional objectives or outcome of learning.

Evaluation signifies a wider, more comprehensive and sustained process of assessing student progress. Thus evaluation is integrated with the whole task of education. The purpose of evaluation is to improve instruction and not simply to measure achievement. Evaluation brings out the factors that is inherent in student growth such as proper attitudes and habits, manipulative skills, power of critical appreciation, understanding, in addition to the conventional acquisition of knowledge.

Education is a process that brings about desirable changes in the child in terms of mental and physical development. Each subject in the curriculum should contribute towards these changes. These changes will form a continuous process during and after the period of education. These changes too would imply the fulfilment of our educational objectives.

An objective is an end-view of something towards which action is directed or a plan for change sought through any activity. Class-room objectives relate to and contribute to the total educational process. Aims are broad objective and are indirect, while classroom objectives are specific, direct and functional. Classroom objectives are the basis for the choice of classroom procedure that provide for suitable experiences to the children, and we can know the extent to which the classroom work has been successful.

An objective becomes tangible and capable of attainment when it is defined in terms of pupils behaviour and content area. Learning experience are the means to attain educational goals. The teacher is to provide the situation, leading to the attainment of any objective.

Learning experiences will differ from objective to objective. Learning will be determined by the action of the pupils.

So evaluation is the process of determining:

(i) the extent to which an objective has been attained,

(ii) the effectiveness of the learning experience provided, and

(iii) how well the goals of education have been accomplished.

The objective (ends), learning experiences (means) and evaluation (evidence) are mutually interrelated. A good evaluation device can secure valid evidence of the desired change of behaviour.

New Type Tests

The examination reform has been the long desired need. Educationists have started realising that no change in education system can be effected unless the examination system is changed. It is also not possible to do away completely with the system of examination and so reform is the only way out. With this aim in view certain researches were carried on and conducted. Now certain new type of tests have been devised. It is claimed that they are more objective and help the examiner to keep away the subjective considerations. These tests are also helpful for the development of the independent thinking and reasoning of the students. Rote memory does not find any important place in these tests. These tests are also connected with the syllabus and curriculum. In fact it is claimed that new type of tests and the old type of tests should be so combined that the results may be good and helpful.

The new system of examination has put forward the following types of tests:

(i) True-false tests.

(ii) Recall tests.

(iii) Multiple choice tests.

(iv) Matching test, etc.

The directions given in this type of test are explicit and devoid of any possibility of misinterpretation. Awarding marks is also objective, easy and simplified. No partial or fractional credit is given for ambiguous answer. There is no provision for awarding marks for hand writing, neatness etc.

True-False Test : It is a recognition test, In this type of test certain statements are given. Before the statement, the words true/ false are written. If the statement is true, student has to tick 'true' and if the statement is false, he has to tick the 'false'.

Example : Enamel is a much harder substance as compared to paint. (True/false)

Multiple Choice Test : It is also a recognition test. In it several alternatives are presented to the pupils from which he must select the one that makes the statement most correct. Such test items can reduce the subjectivity in marking and inter-examiner variability in marking. Such type of tests are quite popular these days and are considered most useful because in this way guessing is minimised and intelligent thinking is encouraged. Some examples of this type of test are:

Example

Q. 1. Deficiency of vitamin D causes:

(a) anorexia

(b) rickets

(c) pellagra

(d) none of these.

Q. 2. The prenatal stage comprises

(a) latency period

(b) oral period

(c) onal stage

(d) puberty.

Reasoning power can play an important role in answering this type of questions and so-called educated guesses should be encouraged. Actually these educated guesses usually are formulated from vague selected ships that are seen or sensed. Very often the person can not explain his reason for selection of correct choices in this type of questions, he just knows. Because there are so many aspects of learning and teaching that are still mysteries to us, teacher should not stand in the way of children learning. Intuition plays an important part in learning as well as in the scientific way of working.

Guidelines for Constructing Multiple Choice Tests : While constructing multiple choice tests following guidelines be followed:

(i) A test item should have a single concept to be tested.

(ii) A test item should be such that it can be used to discriminate a group of students as low, medium and high achievers.

(iii) The statement of test items should be very clear and not ambiguous.

(iv) Be sure that of the possible answer only one answer is correct.

Parts of Multiple-Choice Item : There are generally two parts of a multiple choice test-item, viz., stem and plausible answers. The stem of the test-item contains the statement of the question or problem. There are some important styles of writing the stem of a multiple choice questions. These are:

1. stating the stem in the form of a question.

2. writing the stem as an incomplete statement.

3. writing the stem as a problem to be solved.

The plausible answers are the options available to the student from which he has to choose the correct answer. These are generally written according to following guidelines:

1. Write the answers in such a way that to a student who has not read the topic thoroughly each answer seems to be plausible.

2. Include common misconceptions which an average student holds about a particular learning segment.

3. Options which are true on their own but defy the statement of the problem given in the stem of the test item.

4. Do not provide clues for the right answers.

Completion Test **:** It is a recall type of test. In this type of test students are asked to fill in certain blanks.

Example

(i) Every member of family contributes to—

(ii) The milk teeth are in number—

Example

Match column 'A' with column 'B'

	A		*B*
(a)	Filament	(i)	Toys
(b)	Baby	(ii)	Yarns
(c)	Pregnancy	(iii)	Carbohydrates
(d)	Beetles and Weeril	(iv)	Menstrual period
(e)	Dietary essentials	(v)	Diarrhoea

Matching Test **:** It is a type of recognitions test. In this type of test items two mismatched columns are given one working as problem statement and the other working as options. The questions and answers given in two columns are required to be matched or compared by the students. By giving the pupils two columns of items and asking him to match the related items, the teacher can quickly and easily see if his students recognise the relationship that exists between the items. There is less of stress upon sheer memory or recall of fragmentary information because the materials are presented to the student for his consideration and correlation. This test requires the student to draw a line between the word on the right and a correct one on the left to show the proper relationship.

Because matching tests are focussed mainly to measuring subject matter, it is not always indicative of the pupils ability to perceive the deeper meaning or real understanding of the relationships between the items used on the tests. Stress upon mere verbalization and memory of isolated bits of information should be avoided. Teachers will find it necessary to use all types of testing instruments so as to get a broad picture of the formulation of his children's science concepts.

Short Answer Tests : With all the drawbacks of the short answer tests, there is a wide use for these tests in science education for elementary schools. They are becoming quite popular these days. As the name suggests such questions expect brief, to the point, limited short answers. Generally, the length of answers is specified. They offer the teacher ease of construction and scoring not possible with other types of tests. The tests offer a greater degree of objectivity than other evaluating techniques and the results of tests can be helpful to the teacher for evaluating and reporting children's progress in science education to their parents. With the teacher's guidance, the simplicity of tests can be useful for self-evaluative examinations for the children. Children can also be involved in writing examinations of this type as well as in scoring them. Teachers can be assured that the objective tests being discussed warrant the expenditure of time and effort required to construct them in correct way. Correctly made, administered and interpreted, the short answer test offers many advantages to the teacher, however, they should never be used as sole testing device. They should only be used in conjunction with other types of oral and written tests as well as teacher observation.

Advantages of Short Answer Questions : Some of the important advantages of this type of questions are:

(i) They are easy to design

(ii) Scoring is less subjective and easy.

(iii) The question paper becomes comprehensive i.e., it covers the entire syllabus. The students lose the chance of spotting questions or topics.

Advantages of New Type Tests : Some of the advantages of new type of tests are as under:

(1) In a limited time, we can measure the knowledge of large number of facts acquired by the students.

(2) It helps to test the sense to time sequences and time sense of the students.

(3) It helps to solve the language factor of evaluation. In objective test, students are required to write very little. So it is possible to test the real knowledge of the students.

(4) It is free from the whim of the examiner. His personal desire or whim in making is altogether eliminated. He also cannot commit any mistake at the time of valuation.

Defects of New Type Tests

(1) It is very difficult to frame the questions. An inefficient teacher in history will not be able to frame these questions. The question paper also becomes quite lengthy. It requires a good deal of experience and capacity on the part of the question setter.

(2) There is possibility of guesswork in this type of test in multiple choice test. True false test and matching where the examinees is required to write 'Yes' or 'No' or few signs here and there, there is possibility of guesswork. Hence, it does not help us evaluate properly.

(3) The student does not develop his writing ability. He fails to either a good language or a correct language.

(4) This test does not develop the power of thinking reasoning, problem solving, judgement, and intellect of the students. It only tests the knowledge facts, data time sense etc. It is not very useful for the senior students.

Conclusion

It cannot be denied that evaluation exercises a great influence on the pupil's study habits and the teacher's method of instruction. Therefore, it not only measures the educational achievements but also plays a great role in improving the educational system. The important task before us is to improve the present system of evaluation, at different stages of education. The following suggestions should be taken into consideration for improving the system.

(1) Emphasis should be given on the improvement of question and question paper.

(2) Appointment of paper-setters in Home Science should be made on the basis of competence rather than seniority.

(3) Attempts should be made to improve the technical competence of paper-setters.

(4) Standardization of "Scores" in Home Science should be made.

(5) Mechanization of the process of evaluation in Home Science and completion of results.

The Evaluation

It is a broader term and is not confined to list and measurement only. Through this device the student evaluates her success or failure, teacher evaluates her success or failure and the society evaluates how far the system of education is able to achieve its goal successfully. It is an investigation, an inquiry of testing of knowledge and proficiency of the students personality. Her behaviour and her ability to apply her acquired knowledge in solving various problems. Therefore, evaluation is a test or a rod of measurement.

Education becomes successful through continuous evaluation and so there should be continued appraisal of pupil's progress towards the attainment of predetermined objectives.

Evaluation is a method of interpreting evidence about the all round development of the pupils.

Aims of Evaluation **:** Main aims of evaluation are:

(i) To help in providing more intelligent guidance to teaching learning.

(ii) To help to develop effective curriculum.

(iii) To help in improving the quality of instructions and educative experiences.

(iv) To provide an adequate and objective basis for reporting pupil's progress.

Achievement Tests

Type of Achievement Tests for Home Science

(i) general test,

(ii) diagnostic tests, and

(iii) prognostic tests.

Aim of Achievement Tests : Achievement tests are mainly concerned with the following:

(i) To determine what a pupil's has actually learnt.

(ii) To evaluate teacher's effectiveness.

(iii) To make survey of pupil's performance.

(iv) To help in classification and placement of pupils in a relatively homogeneous group.

(v) To help to know the strength and weaknesses of pupils and to provide remedial measures.

(vi) To form a part of total case history of a pupil.

"A general achievement test is one, designed to express in terms of a single score a pupil's relative achievement in a given field of achievement ....." Hawkes, Lindquist & Mann.

Survey Type Achievement Tests : Such tests are constructed to cover a wide area of learning content and are useful as instruments-

(i) for measuring the total performance in a given field of knowledge,

(ii) for measuring achievement against the standardised norms,

(iii) for measuring the extent of differences in the achievement of various pupils, and

(iv) for comparison of pupil's progress in whole school systems as compared with other school systems.

In survey tests more emphasis is put on general achievement and so their aim is to measure the extent of differences in various pupil's achievement. Survey tests are concerned with maximum achievement.

Prognostic Achievement Test : These tests measure prediction or prognosis as to a learner's expected success in a field of learning in which the learner has not yet participated or has done only slightly. Aptitude tests fall in this category. They are concerned with ascertaining what a learner is able to learn but an achievement test determines what a learner has actually learnt.

Efficient prediction's are possible through combined use of prognostic test, intelligence test and teacher's marks. Prognostic tests can be used to-

(i) lesson the number of failure either by eliminating those who are not prepared to proceed further or by providing basis for a differentiated curriculum,

(ii) help in educational and vocational guidance and in better classification of pupils, and

(iii) find out pupils of superior ability and unusual aptitude and of inferior or average ability.

A readiness test is prognostic. A prognostic test differs from an aptitude test in that the basis of the former is more psychologically complex and less factorially poor.

Diagnostic Test

Diagnostic tests bring out particular weaknesses or strengths of pupils in an area of content. The causes of pupil's weakness are identified and remedial measures taken. In a diagnostic test, we are not concerned with the total score on a test obtained by a pupil, but on the part of scores on the individual items. Such a test includes several of each type of problem at each level of difficulty in order to locate the specific weakness. The theory is that when a pupil fails to answer questions at different levels of difficulty it is assumed that the learner does not know how to do that type of problem at any level of difficulty. The subject teacher can prepare a useful diagnostic test as he/she knows the pupil's difficulties better. Personal interviews along with diagnostic tests discover pupil's difficulties better. A well constructed diagnostic test may serve a diagnostic purpose.

Classroom Achievement Test

In day-to-day teaching the teacher carries on formative evaluation and applies the unit test to know, pupil progress and the success of teaching. At the end of the session, there is summative evaluation through an achievement test covering the entire course. Such tests differ from school to school.

Standardised Achievement Test

A test is said to be standardised when standardisation is done in respect of: (i) content, (ii) procedure of administration, (iii) scoring, and (iv) interpretation of test result.

There are four steps in standardising a test- (a) Planning, (b) Preparing, (c) Trying out, and (d) Evaluating the test. The steps are detailed below:

Planning the Test

(i) Prepare a comprehensive list of instructional objectives in consultation with experts.

(ii) Analyse the content (text books and related materials) and prepare a list of various aspects of content to be tested.

(iii) Go through the old questions and the courses of study.

(iv) Determine the scope of the test and the purpose it is to serve.

Preparing the Test

(i) Prepare objective-based objective type test items covering all aspects of the content. Include 50 per cent extra items than is required in the final test. The items should be critically scrutinised by experienced teachers and other experts. Items should be arranged in ascending order of difficulty.

(ii) Prepare clear instructions for the testees to answer the items. Some practice items may be included.

(iii) Fix up time: The average time taken by a gifted, average and dull student may be the guide in fixing up time.

(iv) Prepare scoring key: One mark for each correct response is to be given.

(v) Make necessary arrangements for administering the test under normal conditions to pupils of varying abilities in different areas. Sample population may be 370 to 372 or more.

(vi) Administer the test, value the answer books and arrange the papers in increasing order of marks.

(vii) Item Analysis: There are different methods. Here, we describe the method suggested by Stanley and Ross.

Arrange the papers into three piles-lower 27 percent, upper 27 per cent (about 100 papers each) and the middle 46 per cent (about 170 to 172 papers). For every single item, W Wh are calculated.

W_i	—	No. of testees answering an item incorrectly or omitting it in the lower group.
W_h	—	No. of testees answering an item incorrectly or omitting it in the higher group.
$W_i + W_h$	—	indicates approximate difficulty value of an item.
W_i	—	W_h - indicates the discriminating index of an item.

The table given in Stanley and Ross is consulted to know $W_i - W_h$ -- A part of the table is quoted below:

Total population	*27 per cent of N* N	*No. of options in an item* (*n*)	*Minimum value of* $W_i - W_h$	*Value of* $W_i + W_h$
243	66	5	12	-
369 to 372	100	2	13	-
		3	14	-
		4	14	-
		5	16	26 to 134

To know exact difficulty index of an item $W_i + W_h$ is multiplied by a constant

100x0/2n (0 - 1) in which n = 27 per cent N and 0 = no. of options.

Items satisfying the criteria of discriminating index and difficulty index are retained and others are deleted.

(viii) The items remained are arranged in ascending order of difficulty. Time is also fixed. Now the final test is ready for try out.

Try Out

(i) The final test is tried out, the papers are scored and marks are tabulated in terms of class interval and frequency.

(ii) ***Statistical Calculation:*** Mean, Median, Mode, S.D., Q.D., are calculated and their significance tested.

(iii) Reliability and validity are determined and interpreted. For reliability split half method may be adopted. The coefficient of correlation gives reliability of half test (or r½). Reliability coefficient of the whole test is obtained by applying the Spearman-Brown prophecy formula:

$$r = \frac{2r\frac{1}{2}}{1+r\frac{1}{2}}$$

In achievement test content validity, face validity, logical validity, concurrent validity are necessary. The external criterion may be school mark or teacher's estimate, etc.

(iv) **Norms:** Norms are provided in terms of percentiles, Z-score, T-score, etc., for interpreting performance (or test scores).

An achievement test may be standardised or non-standardised. Informal objective teacher-made tests meant for classroom use are usually non-standardised.

Principle of Good Evaluation

(1) Evaluation should be made in experience of the child during his growth and development. It should also be a continuous process. At every moment and in each station of child life evaluation is to be conducted.

(2) The teacher should be the examiner. He must do it with the cooperation of children, the headmaster and parent. In addition to terminal examinations, he should take periodical testes, even once in a month. Here attention should be paid to the test of knowledge.

(3) Improvement of questions is also very much essential. In stead of asking essay-type question, New-type test questions should be asked.

(4) Measuring the achievement of the students within the three or four days of annual examination is not scientific. For an examination of Home Science, it is not at all desirable because it deals with more facts than any other subject. To measure the achievement of the students in Home Science, it is desirable that there should be three terminal examination in a year.

(5) Varieties of techniques like questionnaire, checklists, anecdotal records, interviews, reports made by parents etc. should be adopted.

Method of Evaluation

The following three methods should be adopted to know the progress of the students:

Descriptive Reporting : By using this device, the teachers and observers can make important contribution to the teaching in Home Science. Here the teacher is required to maintain a log book to report the respond of the pupils.

Test of Knowledge : This is a method by which the academic achievement of the students can be measured by asking brief and elaborate questions, true false statements multiple choice of matching items to measure their achievement.

Open Questions : It discloses more than matching for multiple choice items but the answer are more difficult to interpret and evaluate.

Techniques of Evaluation

Evaluation is to investigate, inquire and test the proficiency of the students. It is a rod of measurement. Through evaluation, we can achieve our goal of education by keeping a single goal before us. "Educate properly and evaluate scientifically." If we have better question papers improved scoring procedures, better instructional and test materials, we can have better education for our children. There is an increasing awareness towards the improvement of examination at the secondary schools. The common devices like written, oral, practical observational etc. should be applied to evaluate the achievement of the students in Home Science.

Oral Tests : Oral test in Home Science provides an opportunity to the teacher to evaluate the power of expressing, spontaneity of responses and independent thinking. Here, the teacher can test how far the students are able to apply their knowledge. Therefore, the proper arrangement of questions throwing sufficient light upon the unity of study is very much essential.

Essay Type Tests : In essay type tests, the examiners are asked to write about five essays out of eight or ten within three hours. They have to write the answers a bit in detail learnt from the books and class-room instructions.

Short Answer Test : Examiners are asked to answer the questions within limited words. Answers need to be pointed. Here the objective is to evaluate the ability of understanding at large amount of knowledge within a short period by the student.

Objective Type Test : In this test, the examinees are asked to answer a set of large number of short questions in short period. Here they test the knowledge of a large number of facts. Power of judgement by the students is also tested by this device. It is also known as the New-Type-Tests.

Evaluation Devices

Besides the many different teaching devices, there are several other ways to measure the achievement of the students. The most commonly used device by our teachers is the essay type test. An ideal teacher should take the help of other devices besides the essay type test. Pupil's achievement can be evaluated by the devices like laboratory records, class reports, note books, participation in exhibitions, group work and essay type are some of the numerous way in which pupils can be evaluated. If we want to adopt a good evaluation device, we should see that the evaluation is reliable, valid, accurate measure what it is supposed to measure and include items of varying degrees of difficulty. In order to make evaluation stimulating and meaningful, a variety of devices should be used for different purposes.

Let us now discuss some of the important devices under the following heads:

Cumulative Record Card: By the help of this record, one can collect various types of information about the pupils during an academic year. These information include anecdotal records. Personal data, results of tests, questionnaires filled by pupils, home projects reports and such other relevant material. Steps must be taken to maintain these records confidentially.

Anecdotal Records: This is a device by which we can study the behaviour of the pupils. Tolerance, evidences of self-direction, consideration for others, independence in thought and action and other qualities of personality may be obtained in this way. It is difficult to adopt this method in a overcrowded class.

Check-lists and Questionnaires: In an questionnaire, we find a series of question or statement to which the pupils react showing opinions, interests and facts which can give significant information about the pupils.

Diaries: These are records maintained by the students for their observation of own personal experience. By the help of diaries, the teachers can observe the merit of their students.

Written Test: These tests have both subjective and objective aspect. We can test the ability to think, reason, and to plan to solve the problems of life.

Pupil's Behaviour: The behaviour of the pupils in home, school and community can be studied.

Observation: Observation provide an evidence for the study of emotional maturity of the students. Such learning experiences include socio-drama, role playing etc.

The evaluation device differ from one learning devices to another learning device. Let us discuss them under the following heads:

Unit	*Desired Outcome*	*Evaluation Techniques*
Improving home and surroundings	An increased interest in improving home and its surroundings.	Visit of the home of the pupils.
Meals	The ability to choose for oneself and the family meals satisfactory from the stand point of both cost and nutrition.	(i) Written test on principle of nutrition. (ii) Practical test on preparing well balanced meals. (iii) Study of the pupils' records of weights and health status.
Enjoyment of the students	Small skill in providing adequate play experiences for small children.	(i) Judgement of the toys brought by the students (ii) Suitability of the toys according to the age level of the students.

Conferences: In teachers informal conference with pupils, we can study the change the behaviour and practices in home.

Pupil's Performances in the Class: This is quite suitable for Home Science classes. By the help of this device, we can determine the ability of the student to apply the informations learned.

Socio-gram: We can group pupil by the help of this device. The personal and social adjustments of the students can be measure by the help of this device.

Evaluation Procedure

It is very difficult to prepare the objective type test questions but easy to evaluate. For the preparation of this test items the following steps should be taken into consideration:

(1) The important facts principles or generalisation should be which have been taught to the students should be selected.

(2) The actual problems must be selected.

(3) Possible answers should be given.

(4) A list of reasons for the answers to include some adequate some irrelevant, some false some partly true questions to be prepared.

(5) Steps must be taken to arrange the test with the problem first, the direction; followed by conclusions next and reasons last, the latter mixed up in good and poor ones.

(6) To study the strength and weaknesses of the students the evidences must be recorded.

Instruments for Evaluating Scientific Attitudes

One of the most important ways of judging the effectiveness of Home Science teaching is to evaluate the growth of individual children. This is especially true in the areas of scientific attitudes, appreciations and interests. The most suitable techniques for obtaining this information are teacher observation and anecdotal records, tape recordings, rating scales, checklists, interviews, children's work products, essay tests and situation testing.

Teacher Observation and Record Keeping

Following forms have been found as useful aid by teacher as it helps them in making their observations more accurate, systematic and time saving and also provide them with a permanent record of behaviour. These cards can be used for recording anecdotes of children's scientific or unscientific behaviour. As these records accumulate, the teacher can begin to see the direction of growth in behaviour and attitude. It is unsatisfactory to merely say that a child has improved in scientific thinking. We must have some records to substantiate our claims.

Tape Recordings

Use of tape recorder during discussion period can be made for assessing the attitudes and interests of each student. Such tapes of discussions can be analysed by the teacher at his leisure. In many ways the tape recorded sessions have some important advantages over the written records of teachers observations. By use of tape records greater objectivity is possible. These tape recordings can also be used for self evaluation by students. It is expected that such tapes be used for Home Science teaching and learning.

Checklists and Rating Scales

It is a faster but perhaps less comprehensive way of assessing growth in scientific attitudes and appreciations. A sheet is prepared by the teacher and she can use it for his own evaluation also and for modifying his teaching method.

The Interviews

Personal interview of individual or small groups of children enable the teacher to probe into their scientific attitudes and thinking. Interviews may last only a few minutes and the answers given by students are important primarily for the way in which children attempt to answer and not the amount of factual material verbalised. A special session be organised for evaluation of skills in which practical situations are presented for assessing children's scientific thinking and attitude with greater elaboration.

Children's Work Products

Children's work in all aspects of the elementary curriculum provide us with much evidence about their scientific thinking and attitudes. Children's writings, particularly in the intermediate and upper grades, provide enough information about their concepts of the world and their thinking processes. Creative writing allows freedom for the child to explore scientifically and to speculate. Projects and reports provide the format for students to present examples of their thinking.

Situation Evaluation

The teacher can set up situations in which the student is required to find the answer to a practical problem. The student should be unable to supply the answer from memory because ideally he would never have encountered the particular situations. This procedure is quite valuable for assessing problem solving skills.

Evaluating Children's Interests

For success of Home Science teaching programme, the children should strengthen andbroaden their Home Science interests through the evaluation process. Teacher can also analyse children's interest by their choice of books from the class, school or local library. An overview of Home Science interests of children can be ascertained from their selection of reading materials. By keeping a record of reading interest inventories over a period of time, a teacher can see if children increase their voluntary selection of some science books as a result of his Home Science programme. The following types of reading inventories are popularly used:

Name ....

Book and Author ....

Dates read ....

Comments ....

Opinions ....

QUESTIONS

1. What is the purpose of Evaluation ?
2. What are the techniques of Evaluation ?

14

Developing Curriculum

Among the way and means of achieving the set goals of the education curriculum occupies the most significant and central place. If the education in Home Science is to be worth while it has to be planned with the idea of achieving certain aims which represent values attained from its study. Selection of material has to be made with a purpose, that is to be served by Home Science in the general scheme of education. In recent times we find rapid social, technological and scientific changes. We also find significant changes in man's outlook on life.

Need for Planning

The word 'curriculum' is derived from Latin word "curresre" which means to run. Thus, according to its Latin origin curriculum is a race course or a "run-a-way" which one runs to reach a goal as in a race. It is an organised pattern of educational programme, which tries to answer what, how and when. Thus curriculum is an instructional or educational programme by which students can achieve goals and aspirations of life. Curriculum includes the subject-matter and all learning experiences arranged by the school for a particular subject. So curriculum is the sum total of all the experiences of the pupils. It reflects the aims and objectives of teaching Home Science. It should be flexible and should fit the pupils of different age groups.

The needs of life go on changing, so is education, hence we can not go with a static curriculum. The content has to be selected according to changing needs of the society in general and the subject in particular. The curriculum has to be planned and organised in a scientific manner keeping in view the psychological requirements of the students. If the curriculum is properly organised, it enables the students to know the subject matters which they have to study on the other hand it also makes clear to the teacher, the material that they have to teach to the students. It provides the same facility to the examiner.

Since the syllabus contains the experiences of a child and the experiences of each child are different from others, so the syllabus will be different for each student in the school. It is, therefore, quite essential to form a suitable Home Science syllabus.

The Construction

The construction of curriculum of Home Science is a different task, however, it would be easier to construct a syllabi in Home Science if we keep certain points in mind while constructing the curriculum in Home Science.

The important principles that should be given due consideration while constructing a curriculum are as follows:

Principle of Child-centredness : In the modern educational process, we find that the education is child-centered or it is paedo-centerd education. Thus we consider the child as the central factor in the syllabus and our syllabus should be organised keeping in view the present needs, requirements and circumstances of the child. We can impart a meaningful education only by proceeding the child with meaningful experiences. The subject and activities should exercise the powers of the child in construction, creation, observation, investigation, problem-solving and should simultaneously provide for his recreation.

Principle of Comprehensiveness : To meet various needs of the individual and the community, we should have a comprehensive syllabus. It should include a wide variety of subjects to allow options to the pupils for taking up subjects according to their needs and capacities.

Principle of Utility : To make the curriculum useful it is desirable to include in it work-experience. For providing work-experience to the child, we should include some vocational and technical education programme in our syllabus.

Principle of Community Centredness : Since the child is a social animal and has to live with other individuals, thus one of the aims of education in any subject should be to prepare the child to become a successful member of community.

Principle of Integration : It is an important principle that should be kept in mind while constructing a curriculum. This principle of integration means "totality" or "integration" or "total experience" i.e. the experience should be presented as a whole and the different school activities should not be treated in water-tight compartments. To achieve the various aspects of Home Science may have to be organised into integrated units spread over different classes. Thus the unit planning approach may be essential in the organisation of class work.

Principle of Variety and Elasticity : According to modern educational theories, it is desirable to have a flexible and not a rigid syllabus. Such a syllabus should be easily adjustable to the pupil's requirements of different stages.

In the words of Brubacher, "The present syllabus instead of fitting to the child's needs, the child is fitted to the syllabus". This concept needs a drastic change and a change in syllabus accordingly. Since students differ from each other in their ability, interest and aptitude, the curriculum should be constructed according to the needs and interests of the children. Our teaching must be based on latest knowledge about the nature of adolescent girls and their ways of learning.

Principle of Conservation and Creativity : Any effective syllabus must be based on this principle of conservation and creativity. In the syllabus, we should include those subjects and experiences which are helpful in the conservation of past heritage both social and cultural. It should also include such topics that will enable the child to exercise his constructive and creative powers. More emphasis be placed on individual laboratory work and other field experiences.

Excursions and trips should form integral component of our syllabus.

Principle of Good Syllabus : A good syllabus is always related vitally and organically to the community life. It should reflect the local traditions, customs, environments, folk-lore etc. The syllabus should be developed according to various local needs. It should allow the child to come in contact with the life around him. In fact the curriculum should grow out of community life. In a village school, making of different handicraft with locally available cheap materials and economic management of home will be given mort time than in a town school. Similarly preparation of low cost nutritious dishes and preservation of food stuffs in a rural school will not be the same as in an urban school.

Principle of Training for Leisure : While framing a curriculum, it should be kept in mind that it not only prepares the students for work but also prepares them for leisure. If a variety of activities are included in the syllabus then it will help the adolescents to release their pent up energy and emotions in a socially desirable channel.

The Secondary Education Commission appointed by Government of India in 1950 has recommended in its report (1953) the following main principles for curriculum construction at the secondary stage of education :

(i) Principle of relating to the community life,

(ii) The social principle,

(iii) Principle of totality of experiences,

(iv) Principle of training for leisure,

(v) Principle of variety and elasticity,

(vi) Principle of integration.

Present Status

The Secondary Education Commission (1953) states the main objectives of Secondary Education as under:

(i) It should be suitable to the Secular Democratic Republic of India by creating attitudes, habits and qualities of character and citizenship.

(ii) It must try to increase the national wealth by constructive means.

(iii) It should create cultural regeneration.

For achieving these ends in the views of the Commission, the teaching of Home Science can be quite useful. In this respect, the commission further opined that education for girls should be less bookish and more practical. Education should prepare the girls to play their role efficiently as mothers in future and that is why they should be conversant in the way of family life. Special facilities in the study of Home Science should be made available in all girls, schools.

The Education Commission (1964-66) also opined that, "Home Science should provide the pupils with knowledge and skills in house keeping work". In the course of their Home Science work they should be familiarised with the social arrangements. "If greater attention in given to Home Science, with special emphasis on practical work of every day needs and problems, it will help to bridge the gulf between the school and the life of the home and the community, and be a better preparation for a girl's life after school in which home-making will necessarily play an important role. An educated girl who can not run her home smoothly and efficiently, within her resources can make no worthwhile contribution to the happiness and well being of her family or to raising the social standard in her country."

All India Council for Secondary Education included Home Science to be studied in the last three years of secondary education. The All India Secondary Education Council further included Home Science as a part of other subjects to be studied in school. In the present systems girls can opt for Home Science as an individual subject. The government of India and various state governments have encouraged the starting of Home Science sections in schools. At present, a large number of girls are studying Home Science as an important subject.

Present Syllabus

The Present Syllabus in Home Science for the secondary stage is a combination of different branches of Home Science such as physiology and hygiene, health and sanitation, child care and child development, food and nutrition, home management, textiles, clothing and laundry etc. It also consists of a number of practicals on food and nutrition and garment making. The present syllabus is subject centred but it can not be abandoned abruptly because in comparison with experience-centred syllabus the subject-centred syllabus is simple, intelligible and can be easily evaluated.

Defects in the Existing Curriculum

(i) The syllabus is narrowly conceived as it is conventional and static. We are passing through a period of rapid scientific development and revolutionary changes in family life. To meet these demands, we need a most up-to-date syllabus in Home Science.

(ii) The present syllabus is more bookish and theoretical. Various topics have been grouped together under the major head "Home Science". Most of the teachers and students get their information from one text book and so it fails to create any curiosity in the students.

(iii) The present syllabus does not fully conform to aims and objectives of teaching Home Science. It is overcrowded and has very little rich and significant contents. Though a number of periods are allotted for practical work in Home Science yet in practice only a few practical classes are held. It is thus desirable to make the syllabus less theoretical and only such topics which are highly essential for students be included in the syllabus.

(iv) The present syllabus is examination-oriented. It develops a habit of selecting only important question, from the examination point of view, both amongst teachers and students. In this way, only a few topics are learnt and students acquire only a limited knowledge.

(v) The present syllabus in Home Science does not cater to the needs of the students.

(vi) It is not related to practical life and so it fails to develop an interest amongst the students for various topics.

(vii) It has been found that in some universities the Home Science curriculum is not given the same importance as the curriculum in other subjects.

A recent study of the defects in the existing curriculum in Home Science was conducted by the Ohio State University Education team in India and the following defects have been pointed out:

(i) There is a lack of agreement on the purpose and functions of the multipurpose high schools.

(ii) The accommodation and physical facilities available in schools are inadequate.

(iii) Instruments and materials are not available.

(iv) There is an acute shortage of qualified teachers.

(v) No provisions have been made to provide vocational guidance and it is leading to ignorance of girl students in the wise choice of subjects.

R.P. Devdas, the chief Home Economist Government of India, in her book Recent Trends in Education has pointed out, "The existing schools in different schools should be evaluated and revised from time to time in the light of previous experiences and developing needs and trends."

Organisation of the Syllabus

While organising the syllabus of Home Science many factors have to be taken into consideration. Important such factors are:

(i) Content,

(ii) Periods allotted in school time-table,

(iii) The requirements prescribed by the board,

(iv) Other subjects with which Home Science can be correlated, and

(v) The degree of interest that the parents and pupils have in the subject.

To plan the curriculum of Home Science, the following points be given due considerations

(i) Setting of goals for different areas of Home Science in cooperation with students and parents.

(ii) Analysing the goals in terms of outcomes expected or desired behavioural changes.

(iii) Suggesting experiences or activities for achieving the goals.

(iv) Evaluating the outcome to know how goals have been achieved.

(v) Making the required changes in the curriculum in the light of evaluation.

(vi) The specific needs of the community and the pupils as also the resources available.

(vii) Individual differences in the behaviour and ability of pupils.

Procedure and Process

The making of the new programme to the revision of the existing one should never become a mechanical process. There are a number of steps which may be taken in the revision of curriculum in Home Science. These may or may not be taken in the order indicated below. However, it is clear that some of these may be taken concurrently.

1. Obtain the consent and interest of every member of the faculty or department.

2. Obtain administrative consent, interest and support.

3. Describe the scope of revision.

4. Decide upon the extent of revision.

5. In the light of the decision about the scope and extent, set an approximate time limit for the appearance of new programme.

6. Work out a plan of organisation.

7. Work out a plan of procedures.

8. Secure definite information about total enrolment, age distribution, economic and social conditions and any other matter that might throw light on the question of suitable curriculum.

9. Survey the existing curriculum carefully and thoroughly.

10. Survey the work of other systems.

11. Review the research studies in the field of civics curriculum.

12. Survey social trends and current development for the purpose of setting what new aspect for topics of some special significance to community, society should be included.

13. Make a survey of local resources.

14. Make a survey of available resources and equipment of the school.

15. Prepare an outline of an ideal programme.

16. Decide upon objectives.

17. Determine the procedure to be used in selecting the material.

18. Decide upon principles of grading.

19. Decide the plan for organising the material.

20. Decide the contents of the revised programme; shall it contain a mere outline or expanded and detailed subdivisions, projects etc?

21. In dealing with the content decide upon a set of symbols that may facilitate the procedure for making changes e.g.

    D – Delete

    N - New unit, sections and items

    Ex - Expand the present treatment

    Ln - Lessen the extent of present treatment.

22. Appoint a committee on form and style.

23. Inaugurate the new programme with enthusiasm.

24. Evaluate the programme.

QUESTIONS

1. Which are the principles of construction of curriculum?

2. "The advanced modern technology demands a change in the existing curriculum". Express your views and a line of action in this respect.

3. What points will you consider while preparing a syllabus of Home Science for secondary classes and what do you know about the existing syllabus in schools?

4. Discuss the present status of Home Science in Secondary Education.

5. What are the principles of curriculum construction? Suggest some ways to improve the curriculum of 7th class Home Science.

15

Textbooks

In the present educational set up the role of textbook is of prime importance. A textbook gives continuity and cohesion to the teaching process. The report of the textbook committee of the central Advisory Board of Education remarks, "A modern educational system without textbook is as difficult to imagine as Hamlet without the prince of "Denmark". Thus, textbook is an integral part of any educational system. Even in the advanced countries of the world where the technique of teaching learning has advanced a lot, textbook enjoys its respectable place.

In the opinion of experts textbook is an "assistant master in print" and a "tutor at home for self-study" for the students. A good textbook is one which is a source of knowledge arranged systematically and it enables the reader to acquire the needed information quickly. A properly evaluated, a wisely selected and correctly prescribed textbook is an asset both for the students and the teachers. Therefore, the importance of textbook as a tool in the teaching learning process can be hardly ignored especially in a developing country like India.

Meaning of Textbook

Various meanings of textbook are reflected in the following sentences:

(i) Textbook is a record of thinking organised for instructional purposes.

(ii) Textbook is designed for class-room use, carefully prepared by experts in the field and equipped with the usual teaching devices.

(iii) A textbook is a standard book for any branch of study.

(iv) In ordinary usage the textbook is printed, it is non-consumable, it is hard bound, it serves an avowed instructional purpose and it is placed in the hands of the teacher.

Importance of Textbooks

Textbooks occupy a very important place in the teaching of Home Science. They form part of traditional teaching aids. In fact it would be wrong to call them teaching aids. They are means of important knowledge. It is through textbooks that knowledge is imparted to the students. They serve as a guide and means for the teacher as well as the students. It enables the teacher to acquire the needed information quickly. It inspires the students to invent, to discover and to inculcate scientific methods through the use of textbooks the teacher can impart knowledge to the students and can help them to revise the lesson learnt in the class-room. With the help of the textbooks, it is also possible to give home task to the students. If properly used textbooks can go a long way in teaching of Home Science in a successful manner. However, teacher should not depend solely even on the best of the textbooks because even such a textbook omits many details which teacher wants to tell to his students.

The use of textbook is made by the students for completing the preparatory part of an assignment. They also use their textbooks for doing revision of course. Some students also consult and use their textbooks to study at home the demonstration lesson given to them by their teacher in school. In this way textbooks are used to supplement the class work. Textbooks also provide a help to students in correct understanding of basic concepts and principles of Home Science.

Some times text book is more important for the teacher because it will indicate what to teach, how much to teach and how to teach. Hunt says, "In school work in Home Science, the textbook remains after the teacher, the learner's chief support. A well chosen textbook can always be useful adjunct to the efforts of the teacher and a reassurance to the pupil".

Significance in Teaching

Textbooks occupy an important place in the teaching of Home Science. The main reasons for such a position are as under:

Indispensable for the Students : In the class-room, a student mainly depends on teacher's narration, exposition, questions and answers etc. However, students feel a necessity of the textbook for preparing the lesson before they are delivered in the class and a student can appreciate the value of oral lesson delivered by the teacher in the class after acquiring the information and ideas from the text book. As pointed out earlier students also use a textbook at home to do assignments, to prepare for examinations and refers to it during the course of his learning.

Self-teaching, Possible with the Help of Textbooks : Only gifted teachers in Home Science can inspire their students through their lectures which are delivered to impart the knowledge of Home Science. This is the traditional way of imparting knowledge but the main draw back of it is that even the most intelligent student will fail to keep in mind, the whole of the lesson delivered in a class, for a longer period. It is here that the help of textbook is taken by the pupil to have a connected view. Without textbook and teaching materials an efficient teacher with the best planned programmes can not make his teaching successful.

Correct Direction to the Teacher and the Students : Since a textbook is organised in a logical way keeping in view the minimum requirements of the pupils so it is a systematic and comprehensive record of events and experiences. Its use helps the students to save their time and energy. Teachers can also be benefited to a large extent by proper use of textbooks.

A Reference Book for the Teacher : Generally a textbook in used by the teacher for his daily routine work. A textbook provides necessary guide lines to a Home Science teacher for suggesting activities and assignment in the class-room and outside the class-room.

A Laboratory to Experiment and Develop Study Skill : Textbook provides common ground to the students for developing reading skills and for summarizing and analysing the lesson. Pupils also ensure a uniform standard with the help of the textbooks.

Textbooks' Helping the Students of Schools with ill equipped Libraries : In most of our schools the libraries are not upto the desired standards and so they fail to provide sufficient study material to the students and teachers. In such cases textbooks come to their rescue and save them from groping in the dark.

Textbook is Indispensable in the Class-room with Limitation

In our class-rooms we face many a limitation e.g., over crowded classes, lengthy courses etc. The non-availability of teaching aides in one of the major limitations of a Home Science teacher. In solving a number of such difficulties a textbook serves as a panacea.

Inspite of all the advantages listed above a textbook faces many a criticism. It is criticised for being tedious, burdensome, boring, limited knowledge etc. However, it is unanimously agreed that it is most useful instrument for the teacher and students of Home Science.

The Utility

Utility of Textbooks in Junior Classes : In primary classes the students are not very matured. They require textbooks that may serve the under developed mind. In fact textbook should not be used a lot in the primary classes and these should only be sparingly used. Students of primary classes do not require teaching through textbooks. They are more interested in listening. The teaching here should be oral. The textbooks that are used for these classes should be well illustrated. They should contain a good number of charts and pictures. They should be written in such a manner that they serve the psychological requirements of the children of this stage of education.

Textbook in Senior Classes : The textbooks for senior classes should contain facts that are educationally sound and desirable for them. The students at this stage of education are properly developed. They try to learn things in a realistic manner. They can benefit a good deal from the textbooks. The textbooks should be expanded in size and scope according to the changing needs of the society. The arrangement of textbooks should help the students to prepare for their examinations. At this stage of education question-answer method of teaching is desirable. The students may be asked to read the textbooks silently and then questions may be put on the subject matter. For some difficult subject matter, the students may be asked to refer to textbooks.

Characteristics and Qualities

Textbooks in order to be useful should have the following qualities.

(1) Textbooks that are intended to be used should be useful for the students as well as teachers. They should be so designed that on the one hand they may be written according to the psychological requirements of the students and on the other they should serve the purpose of the teacher who wish to impart knowledge to the student in a successful and interesting manner.

(2) The size of the books should be handy. It should be possible for the students to carry them properly. They should not be bulky. This is specially true about books intended for the primary classes.

(3) Printing and get-up of the books be interesting and attractive. They should be printed in the letters that they do not require strain on the eyes of the students. On the other hand they should be correctly and neatly printed.

(4) The exterior of the picture should be attractive. If the exterior is attractive, students would like to carry them and keep them. This is true of the books intended for primary classes.

(5) They should serve the purpose of the subject-matter as well as the aims and objects of teaching. They should be written with the aims and objects of the teaching.

(6) The textbooks should be accurately written. They should present the subject-matter in such a manner that there is no fault in them. The subject-matter, presented therein should be upto date.

(7) The style of the books should also serve the psychological requirements of the students of different stages. Textbooks intended for the students of the primary classes should be written in a story form. In the textbooks meant for higher classes the author may use some other method that is useful for the students of the stage.

(8) The textbooks should continue to keep the interests of the students alive in the subject-matter. The subject-matter should be presented in a simple and lucid style and clear form.

(9) The textbooks should contain all the necessary and relative material required for a particular stage of education.

(10) The textbooks of different stages should be complimentary to each other. Textbooks that are used in primary classes should have some bearing and connection with the textbooks that shall be used by the students in the Junior High School classes. Similarly textbooks that are to be in senior secondary classes should keep in mind the books that have been used by the students in the Junior High School classes.

(11) Textbooks should be free from prejudice. The presentation of the subject-matter should be unbiased. There should be no material which can injure the susceptibility of any class or category of people. They should contain objective description.

(12) The textbooks should contain charts, maps, diagrams etc. as and where required. Without the charts, maps and diagrams etc. the subject-matter cannot be taught properly. It is, therefore, necessary to give place to all these things in the textbooks.

(13) Home Science is a developing subject. Every day we find that new researches have been made in the field to Home Science. Uptodate knowledge of Home Science must be given place in the textbooks.

(14) At the end of every chapter of the textbooks there should be certain questions that may be used for the revision of the subject-matter. Without these questions the textbooks shall not be useful.

(15) If required the textbooks may give a substance of the chapter at the end of each lesson. Such a provision will help the students to grasp the subject-matter properly.

(16) A textbook should be written in simple and small sentences. An effort be made to avoid the use of compound sentences.

(17) A textbook must be selective. While writing textbooks, the author should select the important incidents that influence the community, the adults, the children. The subject matter be treated keeping in view the different stages of education.

(18) The textbook should not be a condensed summary of too many facts. The author should try to keep a balance between quantitative and qualitative development of the textbooks material.

(19) The author should have a considerable teaching experience in Home Science. She should also possess the minimum academic and professional qualifications needed to be a Home Science teacher.

(20) The textbook should be attractive in appearance. Its cover should be artistic and appealing. It should be printed on a good white paper. It should be well bound and free of printing mistakes. It should be reasonably priced.

Prescribing a Textbook

Prescribing a textbook for the pupils is a problem. If we prescribe a single textbook it will limit the knowledge of our students. Generally a number of books are prescribed by Board or University to be used as textbooks. The NCERT prepared textbooks are available upto class XII. While recommending a textbook to her students the teacher should consider the following points to assess the work of the book:

1. Correctness of matter.
2. Purity of language.
3. Simplicity of diagrams.
4. Quality of printing and binding.

Correctness of Matter : In this correction, the standing of the author and the reputation of publishers should be considered. The books written by well known author having a long teaching experience of teaching the subject and possessing requisite qualifications be recommended. It would be much appreciated if certain minimum qualifications and experience for authors is laid down by authorities.

Purity of Language : A textbook that presents the subject matter in a simple, clear and lucid language should be preferred. For textbook in a regional language, the terminology should also be given in English with in brackets. In such books only standard terminology evolved by the Central Ministry of Education and the Government should be used.

Simplicity of Diagrams : Only simple and well-labelled diagrams be given in textbooks. Such diagrams are self explanatory and help the student in properly understanding the subject-matter.

Quality of Printing and Binding : It is desirable that a textbook makes use of good quality paper and the quality of printing, and type of letters in fine. It should be so bound that its binding is appealing to the student.

In addition to the above, textbook is expected to select and arrange the subject-matter in a psychological sequence. The book should follow the aims of teaching geography and should serve as a guide for demonstration lesson as also for individual experiments. Each chapter should start with a brief introduction and a summary of the subject matter be given at the end of the chapter. Some assignments should also be given at the end of each chapter and the assignments should cover such areas as applications to life situations, numerical questions, suggestions for experimental work and projects, objective type tests etc. Heading and subheading be given in bold type. A table of contents be provided at the beginning and a subject-index be provided at the end. Glossary of some important terms be given at the end of the book.

While evaluating a book the teacher should apply objective tests like the following:

1. The contents should be accurate and adequate for the age level and should conform with the syllabus.

2. The concept should not be difficult or ambiguous.

3. The literary style should encourage the student to read the textbook and vocabulary should be well chosen.

4. Photographs should be well produced.

5. The quantity and quality of illustration should be reasonably good.

6. The general get up, binding, size of the book, quality of paper, quality of printing etc. be also taken into consideration.

The Use

The use of textbook is an equally important problem. If the teacher of Home Science follows textbook in his class-room teaching, it becomes easy for the students to understand. Teaching becomes more effective if the teacher adds few interesting anecdote, presents the things in a novel manner. The teacher of Home Science should explain page references and other references to the students. So that student can develop an independent approach. A thorough reading of the textbook is essential to enable the pupils to develop the basic knowledge of Home Science.

Few Restrictions

(1) The textbook is a means not an end in itself. It is an excellent servant but not their master. Students should not feel that they complete their learning only after completing the textbook. It is just a part of their syllabus. Therefore, they should collect information from the textbooks and from other sources.

(2) Loud reading of the textbooks in the class should totally be avoided of facts should be model keeping in view the different stages of education. It will waste the time of the pupils.

(3) A textbook in outline is of no use for primary classes. It cannot create interest among the children. It will lead to memorization of facts and neglect the thought side of Home Science. Therefore, we want narrative textbooks which tell stories in a picturesque manners.

Precautions in Use : While the teacher is teaching the students in the class he should not use the textbooks very much. Textbooks should be used for revising the lesson or for writing out the home task. The teacher may ask the students to read the book at home or in the class and then put questions in order to ascertain whether the students have grasped the subject-matter or not. While teaching, the teacher must put down the substance of the chapter taught on the black-board.

Several methods may be followed by the teachers while teaching Home Science. But we should see that the aims and objectives of teaching Home Science is achieved fully through the use of textbook. Interest towards home work should be stimulated. Properly graded questions should be included in the textbook to realize our aims and objectives of teaching Home Science. An effective use of Home Science textbook will no doubt help use to make the teaching of Home Science meaningful and purposeful.

Nationalization

There is at present a tendency to nationalize publications of textbooks. There are advantages and disadvantages in this. The advantages lie in the possible elimination of inferior stuff and making the books sufficiently cheap. The disadvantages lie in possible omission of important authors and imparting the bias of the powers that be. A viva media policy may be followed to avoid both extremes. They are to introduce those books only which help the easy spread of correct knowledge of Home Science.

Reference Books

Reference books are big standard books that are used by the teachers and grown-up children. Annual Reports, Government Reports, Dictionaries and Encyclopaedia, Magazines etc. form this category of books. These books should be kept in the library for the use of the teachers and grown up students. There should also be rich collection of reference books in the school.

QUESTIONS

1. What is definition of a textbook ?
2. What is a reference book ?

16

Planning of Lessons

A proper planning of lesson is key to effective teaching. The teacher must know in advance the subject matter and mode of its delivery in the classroom. This planning will give the teacher the idea of how to introduce the topic, how to develop the key concepts, how to correlate the concepts to real life situations and how to conclude the lesson.

L.B. Stand conceives a lesson plan as 'plan of Action' implemented by a teacher in class-room. G.H. Green says, "The teacher who has planned his lesson wisely related to his topic and to his class will be in a position to enter the class room without any anxiety, ready to embark with confidence upon a job he understands and prepared to carry it to a workable conclusion. He has foreseen the difficulties that are likely to arise, and prepared himself to deal with them. He knows the aims of his lesson that is intended to be fulfilled, and he has marshalled his resources for the purpose. And because he is free of anxiety, he will be able cooly to estimate the value of his work as the lesson proceeds, equally aware of failure and success and prepared to learn from both."

Importance of Planning

It is a well known maxim that good and effective teaching is, "Causing others to learn". The teacher is expected to create learning situations and organise them in such a way that the child feels inner urge to know, to think and to do. Just as in all other spheres of human activity, it can be achieved by planning, planning makes things easier in every sphere and so the teacher is to think out the best of the teaching procedures so that the results obtained are best. For this, he should follow the maximums of teaching and other accepted principles of education. He also takes the help of various other teaching aids to make the process of learning interesting and concrete. By proper planning a teacher can break up the course into convenient units for each term, each month, each week. In this way teacher will not have to reach through the course towards the end of the session. Planning is also helpful in other ways e.g., it enables the teacher to ensure that he does not emphasize one skill at the cost of some other skill.

Procedure of Planning

For planning a lesson, the following points are duly considered:

(i) The teacher should clearly set the aims and objectives to be achieved by the lesson.

(ii) The teacher should be sure of the position of various teaching aids and other teaching material that is available to him.

(iii) The teacher must give due consideration to the pupil's background and their previous knowledge of the topic.

(iv) The teacher should think of various new activities that could be undertaken.

(v) The teacher should see that the plan of action to be drawn by him should be the best.

With the above things in mind the teacher reviews the material to the taught and then divides it into different sections corresponding to different terms. The work for the term is broken into work for each month and further sub-divided into work for each week and then for each day. The lesson plans are then prepared by the teacher for each lesson. Whatever type and variety of the lesson may be, the teacher can not ignore the following broad principles of lesson planning.

(i) Selection of the suitable subject-matter.

(ii) Presentation of the selected subject-matter in an organised, orderly and effective manner.

(iii) Child activity and participation in co-sharing the educative process.

(iv) Outcomes of orderly procedure and achievement of objectives.

The most important thing in planning lesson is to divide it into following three stages:

(i) Pre-teaching planning,

(ii) Planning during teaching, and

(iii) Post-teaching planning.

In pre-teaching planning are included the preparation of lesson notes. The lesson notes prepared by the Home Science teacher indicate the general lines she will follow and the section into which she is gong to divide the work in accordance with the time schedule at her disposal. In her lesson plan she also indicates the general lay-out of the activities that are to be undertaken by the students. Various steps to be adopted in actual delivery of the lesson are also indicated. A lesson-plan actually is a true picture of what the teacher is going to do in a particular period and what she expects to achieve and how it is to be achieved. It also indicates the previous knowledge of the students that is assumed by the teacher and upon which the topic in hand is based. In a lesson plan the teacher also mention the class, the durations of period, teaching aids to be used and the black board-summary of the lesson. It also includes some recapitulation question and the home-task to be assigned to the students.

Planning during teaching consists of planning black-board work and laboratory work in a systematic way, arranging and presenting the aids in a proper order and planning pupil's activities.

Post-planning activities consist of correction of exercises and home task and recording progress of each pupil.

The teacher must be very clear about the lesson. As the lesson is to be an occasion for the pupils to think, feel and act, as directed and stimulated by the Home Science teacher so the teacher should gauge through the mental and emotional experiences of the class-room in advance and should determine the planning accordingly.

Main Features

In writing a lesson plan, the following points be written down:

1. Date.
2. Period.
3. Class.
4. Duration of period.
5. Subject.
6. Topic.
7. General objectives.
8. Specific objectives.
9. Previous knowledge of the students.
10. Teaching aids and materials to be used.
11. Introduction.
12. Statement of object.
13. Presentation.
14. Generalisation.
15. Recapitulation.
16. Black-board summary.
17. Home-work.

Main Functions

The lesson plan affects the teacher's skill, intelligence, ability and his personality. Following are the chief functions of planning:

1. It delimits the field work of the teacher as well as of the students and provides a definite objective for each day's work.

2. As the goal is determined, the teacher gets impetus to realise his goal.

3. It tends to prevent wandering from the subject and going off the track. It serves as a check on the possible wastage of time and energy of the teachers and students. It makes teaching systematic, orderly and economical.

4. Planning helps the teacher to organise and systematise the learning process.The activities in the lesson are well-knit, inter-connected and associated. The continuity of the educative process is ensured.

5. Planning helps in avoiding needless repetition.

6. Planning helps the teacher to overcome the feeling or nervousness and insecurity. It gives him confidence to face the class.

7. Lesson planning gives opportunities to the teacher to think out new ways and means of making the lesson interesting and to introduce thought-provoking questions.

8. Lesson planning ensures a definite assignment for class and availability of adequate materials for the lesson.

The Essentials

Generally speaking, the following are the characteristics of a good lesson plan:

1. A lesson plan should preferably be written and should not remain at the oral mental stage. Panton writes, "The teacher is strongly advised, at least in the early stages to make a written note of his preparation. Memory sometimes proves a treacherous servant, especially when his attention is divided." It is advisable, however, not to teach from notes. "Excessive reliance upon these may undermine the teacher's confidence so that he can never do without them. If, however, the teacher has occasion while teaching, to refer to his notes, it is better for him to do so openly than to take a surreptitious peep at them. He loses nothing in the eyes of the children by the former method whereas by the second he is likely to be misjudged by his pupils." Writing lesson plan helps in clarifying thoughts and in concentration.

2. The lesson plan should clearly state the objective, general and specific, to be achieved.

3. It should be linked with the previous knowledge. The plan should not let the lesson remain an isolated one. It should have its basis on the background of the class. It should grow out of what the pupils have already learnt.

4. It should show techniques of teaching. It should state clearly the various steps that the teacher is going to take, and also various questions that he will ask.

5. The illustrative aids to be used should be shown in the lesson plan.

6. The materials of instruction or subject-matter should be carefully selected and organised.

7. To motivate the lesson, there must be a provision for audio-visual aids.

8. The plan should be divided into units, but care should be taken to see that the lesson remains an integrated whole and every unit develops from the previous and submerges into the next one.

9. The children must be given enough scope to be active. It should not make them mere passive listeners.

10. The plan should be prepared in such a way as it does full justice to all the students of varied capacities and provides for individual differences.

11. It should show certain routine things. The plan should indicate the duration of the period, the period itself, average age of the students, subject and the class.

12. It should be flexible. The plan is a means and not an end. It is wrong to follow it slavishly. It is an instrument and should be used as such. The teacher should be prepared to change his teaching methods from those as referred to in the plan, if need be.

13. The lesson plan should include the summary of the whole lesson which is to be built up on the black-board with the help of the students.

14. The plan becomes more useful if it refers to references or other reading material. This will encourage the bright

students to read extra books. Care should be taken to suggest only those books which are available in the library.

15. It should include assignment for children. A good lesson plan cannot be thought of without any assignment for the children. The assignment may be in the form of recapitulatory questions or home task.

16. A good lesson plan must have some plan for self-criticism. The teacher should put some questions to himself and find out the answers and judge thereby the effectiveness of the lesson or otherwise.

The Evaluation

The essentials of a good lesson plan have been outlined in the previous section. However, what matters most is the intelligent use of a lesson plan. A lesson plan is not to be followed blindly by the teacher. Certain unforeseen class situations may make it essential for the teacher to modify his plan and for such a situation the teacher should have enough room for flexibility and elasticity in plan.

The teacher will lose much of her originality if she follows her plans rigidly when the real class-room situation demands a slightly modified procedure. An intelligent teacher will not waste any time in adopting the modified procedure because it is not the mechanical pre-determined rigidity of the plan that will determine its work, but the intelligent modification as necessitated by the circumstances. It can be summed up in the following words. In educational journey and its planning, "Derailment may be disastrous, and through running ruinous, make-shifts and stop gap, as demanded by emergency and expediency are all to be admired".

Psychological Units

Education is child centred and the learning process must be based as psychological understanding of a child. Learning takes a well defined course and the teaching process must follow suit. Whatever be the type and form of learning, the teacher is to facilitate it. He has to adopt it to the needs and capacities of the child. It has to be imparted in accordance with various laws of learning if we wish the new learning to be quicker and effective. The teacher has to bear these laws of learning (e.g. Thorndike laws) in mind and to adjust her lesson plan in such a way that the child begins to learn new material presented quite in a spontaneous and natural way.

For such an effective procedure, the lesson has to be divided into certain units or section. The materials within those units or sections may be logically arranged, but the primary units of the lesson are to be based on these psychological laws of learning. Whatever the type of lesson, it is to be divided into certain sections or steps for the development and effectiveness of the learning process. Those stages or steps are known as the psychological units of the lesson. These units of lesson should not be confused with psychological moments. Psychological moments only represent for a definite state of mind when one is ready to embark on any activity, the psychological units stand for the division of the lesson into certain stages or steps to be adopted by or gone through by the teacher.

Various Types

Keeping pace with the changing concepts of education and schooling, it is possible for us to distinguish the following types of lesson that cater to a harmonious blend of personality development. They represent different types of activities that are necessary for their acquisition:

(i) Knowledge Lessons.

(ii) Skill Lessons.

(iii) Appreciation Lessons.

Lesson Plan and Subject

It is necessary for the teacher to be thoroughly prepared before going to the class. The teacher should not only prepare himself but also divide the topic into various subheads. For new teachers, this thing is more important. Really speaking without a properly drawn lesson plan, a teacher cannot do justice to his students. Teachers are given practice in lesson plan drawing. For teachers of long standing it is not necessary to draw Lesson Plans in advance. They can teach the subject even without having a lesson plan before them. However, it shall be useful for them to draw an outline of the lesson plan. For young teachers, it is more or less inevitable. Now-a-days would-be teachers are given a thorough training in the lesson plan drawing. They are made to practise this work while they are preparing themselves for their future assignment. Some of the things which the pupil teachers must keep in mind, while drawing up the lesson plans are as:

(a) Date

(b) Class

(c) Subject and topic

(d) Period and duration.

(e) Name of the institution.

At the top the lesson plan, these things should be put down so that the pupils teacher as well as the students should know the duration in which the topic has to be covered. Name of the class, topic and institution give an idea of the whole situation. After that, following things are to be put down.

General Aims: In these aims and objects, the mental age of the circumstances and other requirements of the student are kept in mind.

Specific Aim: The specific aim of the lesson will be determined in its relationship to any wider purpose or general aim involved. The Home Science teacher should think out and formulate this specific aim in clear cut plan and straight forward manner. General statements like "To exercise the reasoning capacity of the student" or "to include love for one's country" etc. should be avoided in stating the specific aim.

Preparation: To make the pupil's mind ready to receive new knowledge and welcome it, this step is very essential. In this step of preparation the previous knowledge of the student be tested and then the present topic may be linked with the previous knowledge of the students. If the teacher succeeds in linking the present with the past, in the field of knowledge, he succeeds. By linking the present subject-matter with the previous knowledge of the students, useful results can be achieved.

Introduction: At this stage that a teacher prepares students for studying the subject or the topic, he puts certain questions to the students and with the help of these questions prepares a proper background. There may be various methods of preparing the background including Question Answer method. In the concluding questions of this step, the topic and subject matter which is to be taught, may be made perfectly clear.

Statement of Object: After the 'introduction' the teacher must explain the students the subject that is to be taught.

Main Lesson: Under this heading the topic is actually presented. Teaching is properly organised and the lesson is divided into various subheads. While doing all this, it should be kept in mind that certain factors may be included in them.

To keep the interest of the students alive it is wise for the teaching to put certain questions to the students while the process of teaching is going on. With the help of these questions, it shall be possible to develop the lesson.

In case of presentation of long units, the unit may be further subdivided into sub units. After finishing each sub-unit the teacher should find out if the material taught has been assimilated by the students. Here we emphasise that Home Science teacher should realise that assimilation and comprehension are very slow processes and the child takes her own time. The ideas can not be made clear to the students by simply enunciating or telling them to the students. The Home Science teacher must dilate upon, explain and illustrate them and then see that they have been correctly grasped.

This step of presentation is also referred to as development because it is here that development of knowledge takes place.

During presentation stage the Home Science teacher should bear the following principle in mind:

Principle of Selection and Division: The Home Science teacher should select the material that is to be presented very wisely and judiciously according to the suitability of the children. What is to be presented and how much is to be presented are the two basic questions that must be given a priority attention. The teacher should also decide how much she is to tell and how much the pupil are to find for themselves, i. e., she is to divide thoughtfully the share of participation in the educative process.

Principle of Successive Clearness: While dividing the lesson into different sections, the teacher should see that well connected and proper sequence is maintained. She should assure herself that unless the proceeding knowledge is clear to the students, she should not rush for the succeeding knowledge. Sequential and successive clarity must be strictly adhered to.

Principle of Absorption and Integration: Each section or item of the new knowledge or material at first should be exclusively attended to. Then it should be integrated with what has preceded, for example: In a series of sub-sections a, b, c, d, etc. it is to be dealt with first in itself then integrated with a, similarly c first in its own field, then with (ab) and so on. For example we are dealing with the rainfall of a particular place. We integrate this knowledge with the rainfall of the province, later with the country or the region and then with the world-belts or regions of a particular rainfall, etc.

Association of Comparison: The new knowledge to be learnt is to be compared and contrasted and associated with old to get a new knowledge. Knowledge is not like piling up bricks after bricks, it is like a tree that grows. Children grow in knowledge through comparison and association. Educationists are of the view initial stock of knowledge grows through the following three ways:

(i) Further and new experiences.

(ii) Association of new facts.

(iii) Education of new relations between facts.

New facts or knowledge that is to be presented to the children should be due in such a way that there takes place the growth in knowledge and becomes one with the children's previous knowledge or facts learnt.

In this process Adamson points out, "The teacher has neither place nor part". Her part lies in the preliminaries, she is to arouse interest, effort them with opportunities for gaining experiences and associating new facts with old knowledge. When new knowledge is presented to the students, they are asked to observe it very carefully and to compare it with another set of facts they already know, to associate it with the old and thus to turn it into something new. It is a blend of old and new giving rise to a new.

Such comparison and association step is very important while dealing with a purely Inductive Lesson, such as, arriving at a formula in Algebra, generalising rules in Grammar, establishing laws in Science.

Association and comparison is sometimes not considered as a separate step, but a part of the presentation step. Its importance lies in educing new relations from a combination of the old and new.

Generalisation: When the mind comprehend new knowledge, it compares constants with what is already present and only then are arrived at general ideas and establish some laws or formulae. This step enables the Home Science teacher as well as the taught to systematise the knowledge learnt.

In subjects like Mathematics, Science or Grammar, etc. where we are dealing with inductive type of lessons, the students are generally required to establish some formula, law, generalisation or the rule. The approach is always through particular examples. They observe and compare facts and find the agreement among them or the common element is discovered and thus they let to frame a general law or principle. The Home Science Teacher's function is to enable the pupils to draw out the generalization from the relevant data well-collected and arranged. As far as possible, the children should themselves draw out the conclusion through the shifting of the whole material before them. Of course, sometimes, the pupils, generalization may be either incomplete or wrongly stated, the Home Science teacher should guide them to correct and complete it.

Sometimes inexperienced teachers through their leading questions and unwise suggestions, divulge the conclusions or generalization, which ought to be discovered by the pupils themselves. The Home Science should not be impatient to some children from the trouble of thinking. The formulation should be the work of the students, the teacher is only to make it exact. Generalization is of little value to take the children if it is not the product of their own thinking, reflection or experience. Therefore, it is constantly to be borne in mind that at this stage the Home Science teacher is to recede into the background.

Application: Knowledge without being applied is as useless as knowledge incompletely or defectively acquired. T. Raymont has beautifully pointed out, "The mere acquisition of rules, precepts, principles, definitions and laws make directly for pedantry rather than for healthy mental development."

It is essential that when some truth has been established, it should be verified through its application to further examples. Inductive process for establishing generalisation must be followed by deductive application. It is a natural sequence. The learner is always desirous and anxious to make use of the generalisation, rules or formulae to arrive at, and to see these really work in new situations. It is a fundamental law of psychology that consolidation of knowledge only takes place when the knowledge learnt is oppositely applied to similar situations. Knowledge becomes clear and a part and parcel of the mental make-up when it is put to use and verified. When further applied to particular situations or facts, the generalisations, rules or principles gather further evidence and are thus fully and securely established.

Recapitulation: If the lesson is imparted according to the Herbartian Scheme, the question of recapitulation is not to be overlooked. Recapitulation is merely a revision or repetition of the knowledge learnt in the lesson, or it is a sort of going over again and the salient or important features of a lesson are revised whereas application is the use of the knowledge learnt, recapitulation is the exercise of memory or retentivity of knowledge. Application also requires a good deal of mental activity to think and apply the knowledge learnt to new situations.

Recapitulation may take place either at convenient sections of the lesson to revise the main facts taught therein (such type of recapitulation is called as Sectional Revision), or it may come at the end of the lesson. It is asking the children to 'tell back' or reproduce what they have learnt. It may incidentally enable the students to express themselves. Though ultimately we may be aiming at original expression yet the value and importance of facile reproduction cannot be gainsaid. Children should be given adequate practice in reproducing the material learnt before they are capaciated to give all original expression.

Forms of Application: The application of the knowledge learnt may take a variety of forms. The plan of putting the knowledge learnt to see in the form of solving some problems in Mathematics, which has been traditionally confined to this subject only, should be extended to all types of knowledge disciplines. The pupils may be drawing a map or making a model. They may be writing an essay, or making some experiments or doing some practical work. They may be applying the geographical knowledge learnt to the description of an imaginary journey. Children may be given some constructive or creative exercise in which they may exhibit their originality. New type test may also be usefully set to the students.

Model Lesson Plan

Date	Time: 40 minutes
Class - VIII	Period
Subject- Home Science	Topic: Food and Nutrition.

General Aims

1. To foster in the pupils a wholesome attitude towards Home Science.

2. To enrich and expand the knowledge of the pupils in Home Science.

3. To provide the students knowledge about food and nutrition through the medium of Home Science for healthy family living.

4. To develop in the pupils good food habits.

Specific Aims

1. To impress on pupils how like air and water food is basic to our existence.

2. To provide them with necessary information about the function of food.

Previous Knowledge : Students are familiar with some types of foods.

Introduction

To introduce the lesson, the teacher should narrate how food is the primary concern of man in his physical environment. Food or lack of it has influenced a great extent to the future of man. One must eat to live and what one eats affects to a high degree one's ability to keep healthy, to work, to be happy and to live well. Nutrition is the Science of food.

Presentation

At this stage, the teacher should start with the importance of food for our existence. Simple food preparation, nutritional values hygiene of food etc. in the following ways :

	Matter	*B.B. Summary*
1.	Problems of food	How India is facing food problem?
2.	Food Practices	How they buy their food? How meals are planned? How much food preparation is being done?
3.	Nutritional Standard	How nutritional standard effects us?
4.	Balanced Meal	An Exhibit of balanced meals using models and preserved foods, colourfully and attractively arranged will stimulate interest.

Comprehension Tests

The teacher should ask some short, simple and direct questions to the pupils to test their power of comprehension of the ideas contained in the portion he taught.

Application

Teacher should ask some new-type-test to the pupils to test how far they have been able to assimilate the knowledge imparted to them and how far the aims of teaching Home Science have been achieved.

QUESTIONS

1. Give various principles of lesson plan. Draw a lesson plan for a secondary class in the field of child care.

2. What is the importance of lesson-planning in teaching? Plan a lesson for class VII.

3. What are the advantages of preparing lesson plans?

17

Record Maintenance

Every institution has to maintain records, reports and registers which show its origin, growth and development, its present and past conditions, its efficiency and usefulness and its aims, aspirations and achievements. The school being a social institution, is answerable to parents of the students, to local and state governments which maintain it, to society of which it is an organised agency and to pupils who must be developed physically, intellectually, morally, socially and culturally through its programmes, functions and activities. All this makes the keeping and maintaining of records very necessary. It is must for the effective crunning of a school and also an important aspect of administration.

Need and Importance of School Records

The following points highlight the need and importance of school records and registers :

Legal requirements: The Education Department has prescribed certain records and registers to be maintained by each school otherwise they are disaffiliated. Every school is required to keep an accurate and complete account of each pupil and submit periodic reports. Such reports contain facts and figures about total number of students in the school, in each class and section, average daily attendance, number of students newly-admitted, withdrawn or transferred, students belonging to rural and urban areas, scheduled castes, tribes, backward areas and classes; distribution of students age-wise and sex-wise; income from fees, grant-in-aid and other sources, expenditure, staff statement, details regarding school equipments etc. These facts and figures are very important because they form the basis for distributing state grants and aids to private schools.

Financial Needs: The schools have to maintain facts and figures to justify their budget and financial needs. These data are utilized for planning future programmes. These are submitted to the higher authorities in the beginning of the school year.

Administrative Needs: Maintenance of records and registers help in wise and proper planning for efficient school organisation and administration.

Research Needs: Records supply comprehensive data to those who are engaged in educational research and reforms. They get the clear view of how funds are spent on various items. In this way, they discover financial loop holes and how economy and savings can be effected in the efficient management of the school system. It enables the school authorities to introduce new educational reforms and provide new educational facilities according to the demands of time and situation. Such research data helps in the statistical analysis and interpretation of policies and programmes.

Assessment of Institutional Programme: School records show the progress made by the students in curricular and co-curricular activities, work done by the teacher, the guidance given by the headmaster and other authorities, benefits of library and laboratory and their utilisation. Knowledge of educational achievements can be had from examination register. Their physical development can be known from medical records kept in the school. Such an evaluation will enable the headmaster, teachers and educational authorities to make any improvement in their instructional programmes and co-curricular activities.

Guidance Needs: Students can be given proper guidance on the basis of their school records. The records show the achievement and deficiencies of the students. They are guided accordingly. Guidance regarding their future life can be based on their previous achievements.

Required for All-round Development: Main aim of education is the all-round development of the child. This is to be done through their participation in various curricular and co-curricular programmes of the school. The school can perform this responsibility if there is regular record of student's progress in the desired directions.

Needs Regarding Parents' Co-operation: With the help of school records, the progress report of children is prepared and sent to their parents. On the basis of their report, parents' cooperation concerning the progress of their children can be sought. This helps in establishing closer contacts between the home and the school. The development of good home-school relationship is essential for the maximum development of the child.

Efficient Functioning of the School: School records and registers are helpful in efficient functioning of the school. All the school personnel-teachers, students, supervisors etc. are conscious of the fact that their work, achievements and deficiencies are properly recorded. They make efforts to improve upon their previous records.

Responsibility to Parents: Parents send their children to schools for education. They pay tuition fees and other charges, where education is free; they pay indirectly in the form of taxes. Thus it is duty of the school to keep the parents informed regularly about the achievements of their children. This is possible if regular record of students' progress is maintained in the school.

Responsibility towards Society: Schools have a responsibility towards the society also. Today's children are adults of tomorrow. School is to prepare future citizens for the progress of the society. Thus, the education and desired development of students are the main functions of the schools. In order to furnish this information to all the concerned or interested parties, it is essential to maintain complete and systematic record.

Responsibility towards Government: Education expenditure is taken by the centre and state government. The school has to show in the record that proper education is provided to the students and government money is properly utilized. Schools who have to obtain the grants have more of the responsibility. They have to satisfy the departments so that grant given to them is utilized for appropriate purpose and their institutions function efficiently.

Responsibility towards School Management: For the conduct of private schools, the managing committees are there. They spend huge resources on the efficient running of the institute. In this regard, they want full details of the accounts and instruction from the school. Thus, it becomes necessary for the institute to maintain the records.

Responsibility towards the Students: To provide for the balanced development of the children, a total account of their physical, mental, social, moral and cultural development should be maintained from time to time. Thus, they must keep the regular record of progress of students in various school programmes.

Thus, it becomes clear that school records are useful to students, teachers, parents, researchers and all other related to the school. Educational aims cannot be achieved without proper records.

The Advantages

According to Chamberlain and Kindred, following are the advantages of maintaining school records :

Advantages to the Schools

Records help the school

(i) to locate each pupil quickly.

(ii) to have available the facts significant about each student.

(iii) to explain and remove undesirable conditions.

(iv) to find if all legal requirements are met.

(v) to determine if any administrative or other changes are desirable.

(vi) to make important investigations and case studies possible.

(vii) to find if school funds are adequate and wisely expanded.

(viii) to reduce retardation and failure to a minimum.

Advantages to the Teachers

Records help the classroom teachers

(i) to know pupils when the schools year begins.

(ii) to determine what work a pupil is capable of doing.

(iii) to provide learning activities suitable to each pupil.

(iv) to formulate a basis for the intelligent guidance of pupils.

(v) to explain the behaviour characteristics or unhappy conditions of any pupil.

(vi) to make possible the development of unusual capacities or exceptional talents.

(vii) to identify and make proper provisions for the mentally slow pupils.

(viii) to make assignments to committee work and monitorial-positions.

(ix) to make periodic reports correctly and in time.

(x) to be properly informed when conferring with parents and others about a pupil.

Advantages to the Pupils

Records help the pupils

(i) to receive fair consideration in his classification.

(ii) to do his best in making a record.

(iii) to make progress in accordance with his ability.

(iv) to secure development of his natural capabilities.

(v) to secure transfer of correct information to other schools when desired.

(vi) to receive proper adjustment and guidance.

Objectives of Maintaining Records

From the analysis of records maintained in the high schools, it has been seen to contribute to five major purposes :

(i) to assess in guidance, classification and placement of students.

(ii) to improve class room teaching methods by giving the teacher information regarding the individual differences of pupils.

(iii) to motivate student's work.

(iv) to help in educational research.

(v) to meet requirement of, and provide basis for reports to state and local authorities.

Essential Requisites of School Records

The records to be effective, purposeful and useful must maintain certain qualities for definite tasks e.g. selection, use and maintenance of individual records of pupils. The school records should have the following requisites :

Completeness: All records and registers should be up-to-date. These should be maintained in such a way that clerical work is minimum. These should not consume much time of the head of the institute as he is to attend so many other things like class-teaching, organisation and supervision of school activities. No entry should be left blank. There should be continuous record of a child. In case he transfers to another school, his record should follow him.

Accuracy: The information contained in the school record should be accurate and well organised. All records should be true, genuine, reliable and valid. Records are the indications of honesty and integrity of the person maintaining it. The accuracy of the records can be maintained by regular checking.

Utility: Only relevant and useful information should be recorded. It should serve the purpose of reference in future. Irrelevant information would only mislead a person.

Simplicity: School records should be simple, flexible and up-to-date. While consulting these should be easy to consult and understand.

Easily Available: School records are important documents. These should always be available in the school and should be kept at a safe place under lock and key. They should never be taken outside the school.

Easy Maintenance: School records and reports should be easy to maintain. They should require minimum of time and energy for making entries.

Systematic Maintenance: School records should be systematically maintained and located so that the staff members can utilize these to the greater extent. Records should not have errors, cuttings, over lappings and duplication. Separate files should be kept for the separate records. It helps in easy consultation when required.

Space for Additional Entries: There should be some space left under certain headings so that the additional entries could be adjusted and explained. The records regarding students achievements should be entered on the specific period of the year.

Records and registers should be carefully designed, properly kept, strategically located and should contain accurate, complete and useful information.

Important Factors

For keeping proper records, the following points should be kept in mind :

1. Records should be neat and clean. If there is any cutting it should be signed by the head of the institution.
2. Records should be up-to-date.
3. Records should be maintained by the teacher concerned, eg., records of Home Science laboratory should be maintained by the Home Science teacher.
4. There should be list of all registers in the school. One copy should be with the head and other with the clerk.
5. Every record and register should have headings, eg., name of the school and department, serial No. of the register etc.

6. The pages of the register should be marked in ink.

7. The head of the institute should certify the number of pages of the register.

8. The records should be kept in systematic order.

9. Records should be kept under lock and key.

10. All efforts should be done to keep the accurate records.

Log Book

Educational rules require the maintenance of a log book. It is socially designed for the purpose of inspecting and supervisory authorities. They enter their remarks, observations and suggestions regarding the progress on the achievement of the school in both academic and non-academic activities. In public schools, this serves the purpose of diary. Special incidents or achievements, introduction of new books and remarks by distinguished visitors are also entered in the log books. It should contain a complete record of events and should furnish material for the history of the school. Log book contains detail of apparatus or courses of instruction, adoption of new or modern techniques of teaching, appointment of new teachers, provision of any new facility in the school, and plan of lessons approved by the inspector, the visits of the inspecting officers and other distinguished persons interested in education, closure or change in the working hours of school or account of epidemic diseases, and any other deviations from the ordinary routine of the school, or any special circumstance affecting the school that may deserve to be recorded for future reference or any other reason. All such entries in the log book should only be made by the head of the institution. Since log book is a school diary, it should contain only facts and figures and not expression of opinion about these facts. It is a permanent record for future reference.

Stock Book

It is important school record concerning the movable property of the school. The head of the institution is responsible for the property of the school. There should be stock book in which furniture, teaching appliances and other items purchased from time to time are written. It is also called the property register. This register contains entries such as (i) the date of purchase (ii) the name of the article (iii) the number of articles purchased (iv) their price (v) name of the firm from which purchased (vi) the authority ordering its purchase.

Since head of the school is the custodian of school property thus he should maintain these registers up-to-date. These should be checked by the head at least once a year. Verification should be recorded, entered, signed and action should be there if there is some difference. Checking of furniture is simplified if separate inventories of articles of various rooms and laboratories are prepared and kept up-to-date. Every class in-charge is responsible for the classroom property. New insertions if required, should be made with the permission of the head of the school. Whenever an article is damaged and is rendered useless, it is destroyed or auctioned with the permission of the head of the school. Another file containing the orders of the headmaster regarding destroying or auctioning such articles is maintained. In Home Science department, entries of articles should be listed under the different headings like relating to Foods, Clothing, Textiles, Laundry, Home Management, Child Development etc. Laboratory and Library Stock registers are separate. Stock checking should be made the annual feature of the school.

Account Book

It is a record of all money transactions, carried through from day to-day and month to-month in the school. All money received by the school from fees, fines, funds, donations, scholarships, stipends, grant-in-aids and ad-hoc grants from the government treasury are entered on the credit side while all payments made by the school i.e. staff salaries, provident fund, equipment bills, property bills, student fund bills, telephone bills, building rent, contingent expenditure, deposits made in the treasury, bank and post office etc. are shown on the debit side. While writing cash book the following points should be considered :

(i) Balance must be brought forward on each new day.

(ii) Closing balance and opening balance should be written neatly and in red ink.

(iii) Balance should be always as plus 'balance' and not 'minus balance'

(iv) Day's account should be closed with signature of the head of the institution to avoid any alterations.

(v) The entries in the cash book and corresponding entries in other registers should tally e.g. Contingent "Registers, Union Account Register, Admission Fee Register, Medical Register, Games Account Register etc. and also with the remittances and withdrawal in the pass-book and copies of the challans.

Cash book is completed by the ledger. All entries made in the cash-book are carried to the ledger in their respective items, columns and accounts. Such a procedure provides assistance in the preparation of annual accounts, annual statistics and annual returns.

QUESTIONS

1. What are the advantages of maintaining school records? Which points should be considered while maintaining the records ?

2. Write short notes on the following :

   (a) Stock Book

   (b) Account Book

3. How can you maintain the records of log books and account books correctly and how they can help a Home Science teacher?

4. What is the importance of maintaining records in a school? How can you maintain account books?

18

The Correlation

The major aim of education is the unification of knowledge existing in different branches of learning. It is not desirable to impart education in isolated manner. The knowledge has to be knit together through correlation.

According to Herbert Spenser, the power of mind does not depend upon the amount of information accumulated in pieces not related to one another, but is rather on well-organised system on which all these pieces of knowledge or information are taught, showing their relationship with one another. This is known as principle of correlation.

Chatham once remarked, "I have learnt all my English History from Shakespeare's play". This statement refers to the correlation of subjects and importance of correlation.

Correlation makes teaching meaningful and effective for the pupils. It establishes reciprocal relationship that exists among different subjects.

Various Types

Correlation is of many types. Important of these are:

(i) Incidental Correlation,

(ii) Systematic Correlation,

(iii) Correlation with the activities of daily life,

(iv) Correlation of old and new knowledge,

(v) Correlation of different branches of Home Science,

(vi) Correlation of Home Science with different subjects.

Incidental Correlation : This refers to the correlation of Home Science and other subject by the teacher whenever he finds such an opportunity while teaching Home Science. This is not a planned correlation and so it needs no prior preparations.

Systematic Correlation : In this type of correlation, the plan for correlation of Home Science with other allied subject is planned by the teacher in the beginning of the session, e.g., Health education is an allied subject of Home Science and they should be grouped together. Such a planning should do justice to all the allied subjects.

Correlation with Life Activities : Home Science can not be taught in isolation. The utility of this subject is not confined to the classroom or the school only. It has an important bearing on various aspects of life. As far as possible while teaching Home Science, a reference should be made to its use in actual life whenever we go out for shopping and purchase certain things we get them measured and weighed. In this activity Home Science plays its role. The pupil should, therefore, be explained the utility of Home Science in daily life. While teaching the common elements in what is learnt and the life situations to come in future should be pointed out. This is the doctrine of identical components for transfer of learning.

C.T. Lewis says, "Knowing begins and ends in experience, but it does not end in the experience in which it begins".

Correlation of Old and New Knowledge : Various topics in Home Science be arranged in such a manner so as to correlate old knowledge with new knowledge. In Home Science it can be done at the introduction stage. While asking introductory questions, the teacher should test the previous knowledge of the students and try to build up new knowledge and thereby correlating the old knowledge with the new knowledge.

Correlation of Different Branches of Home Science : There are many a well-recognised branch of Home Science e.g. home management, textile and clothing, food and nutrition etc. Truly speaking all these are correlated very closely and an attempt should be made by the Home Science teacher to correlate them while teaching. For example, while teaching 'child care and mother craft' a correlation be done with `food and nutrition'. An effort should be specially made to correlate the teaching of Home Science with new fields of education such as population education, continuing and non-formal education, agricultural extension, adult education and social work. If this correlation is made clear, they shall be benefitted by it at future stages besides the present.

Correlation with Different Subjects

Correlation between Home Science and Literature. The job of creating a real home is quite difficult and this difficult job always falls on the shoulders of the housewife. She is expected to provide for good health, happiness, comfort, convenience, love and affection to all members of the family. She can perform it well if she has a loving nature and is emotionally attached towards the family. In literature we find much about emotions, feelings, love etc. and these are used in practice in Home Science. Mothers can teach their children nursery rhymes and group song from the study of literature. Hence Home Science is related to literature.

Correlation between Home Science and Economics. Home Science is also known as home economics. Home Science has now moved out of home to reach the community and the nation. It is closely correlated to economics inside the home, while dealing with both material and human resources. All these resources are an integral part of family and in this Home Science takes the help of economics.

Correlation between Home Science and General Science. There is a close correlation between Home Science and general science. This can be observed in a large number of topics such as nutrition, textiles and clothing, cooking, laundry, Health and Hygiene etc. When we are teaching in Home Science class about food adulteration, malnutrition, various foods and their nutritive values or about various diseases we have to make use of our knowledge of general science. Similarly, while teaching about plants and their cultivation, fertilizers etc. the Home Science teacher makes use of the knowledge of general science.

Correlation between Home Science and Physical Education. Physical education is concerned with the knowledge needed for improvement of health and maintenance of good health. Such a knowledge is quite essential for the home-makers and in Home Science a knowledge about personal hygiene, hygiene of clothing, importance of physical exercises etc. is imparted. Thus, we find a good deal of correlation between Home Science and physical education.

Correlation between Home Science and Moral Education. The moral education is an essential part of a child's education. Highest love for man is morality. Moral values are learnt by the child since his infancy in his home and surroundings in some informal way. However, a formal education in moral values be imparted to the child in his Home Science classes.

Correlation of Home Science with Arts, Music and Crafts. In Home Science we teach the pupil about painting, colour combinations in dressing decoration handicraft, history of sculpture etc. In all these fields we can easily bring about a correlation of Home Science with arts, crafts etc.

Correlation between Home Science and Mathematics. Home management which is an important aspect of Home Science depends on several managerial process such as planning and assembling resources, directing and controlling work processes and evaluation of results achieved. All these processes are quite dependent on each other. A proper management requires a proper use of money, materials, time and energy to achieve the goals of management. It is essential to correlate Home Science with mathematics. If a middle class family plans to save some money for some social function they have to make adjustments here and there in their budget and for this they have to make use of their knowledge of mathematics similarly, while making daily purchases we have to use our mathematical knowledge.

It can be easily seen that a knowledge of mathematics is required for all our activities that we undertake in household management, cooking, laundring, health and hygiene etc. Thus, we find that there is a close correlation between mathematics and Home Science.

Correlation between Home Science and Social Studies. In social studies, we are interested to study about man and his interaction with other people, with other institutions, with the earth and with goods and services. In this way we intend at the development of a well informed, intelligent person who is keen to accept responsibility of the home as of society. Home is the basic unit of society and of social sciences. In Home Science, we also deal with home as the basic unit interlinked to community. So Home Science and social studies are closely correlated.

Conclusion

From the above discussion, it follows that Home Science is intimately related with various other branches of knowledge. It plays an important role in the study of other subjects. It is both a science and an art. However, while making a correlation of Home Science with other subjects it be kept in mind that the correlation is done in a natural setting and never by force just for the sake of correlation. The experiences provided in Home Science class should be such as to draw applications from other subjects and a study of Home Science should help the students to learn all other subjects with ease.

Correlation helps in teaching various subjects in a better way in association with one another and helps to avoid repetition and contradiction. With its help knowledge is revealed as a unity and not as a bundle of separate subjects.

QUESTIONS

1. "Home Science has its roots in the basic sciences subject." Support your answer with examples.
2. What is the meaning of Home Science and how it is related to other subjects of school?